MW01121002

Microsoft® Office
Access™ 2007

Level 1 (Second Edition)

Microsoft® Office Access™ 2007: Level 1 (Second Edition)

Part Number: 084887
Course Edition: 1.10

NOTICES

DISCLAIMER: While Element K Content LLC takes care to ensure the accuracy and quality of these materials, we cannot guarantee their accuracy, and all materials are provided without any warranty whatsoever, including, but not limited to, the implied warranties of merchantability or fitness for a particular purpose. The name used in the data files for this course is that of a fictitious company. Any resemblance to current or future companies is purely coincidental. We do not believe we have used anyone's name in creating this course, but if we have, please notify us and we will change the name in the next revision of the course. Element K is an independent provider of integrated training solutions for individuals, businesses, educational institutions, and government agencies. Use of screenshots, photographs of another entity's products, or another entity's product name or service in this book is for editorial purposes only. No such use should be construed to imply sponsorship or endorsement of the book by, nor any affiliation of such entity with Element K. This courseware may contain links to sites on the Internet that are owned and operated by third parties (the "External Sites"). Element K is not responsible for the availability of, or the content located on or through, any External Site. Please contact Element K if you have any concerns regarding such links or External Sites.

TRADEMARK NOTICES Element K and the Element K logo are trademarks of Element K LLC and its affiliates.

Microsoft® Office Access™ 2007 is a registered trademark of Microsoft® Corporation in the U.S. and other countries; the Microsoft® Corporation products and services discussed or described may be trademarks of Microsoft® Corporation. All other product names and services used throughout this course may be common law or registered trademarks of their respective proprietors.

Copyright © 2008 Element K Content LLC. All rights reserved. Screenshots used for illustrative purposes are the property of the software proprietor. This publication, or any part thereof, may not be reproduced or transmitted in any form or by any means, electronic or mechanical, including photocopying, recording, storage in an information retrieval system, or otherwise, without express written permission of Element K, 500 Canal View Boulevard, Rochester, NY 14623, (585) 240-7500, (800) 478-7788. Element K Courseware's World Wide Web site is located at **www.elementkcourseware.com**.

This book conveys no rights in the software or other products about which it was written; all use or licensing of such software or other products is the responsibility of the user according to terms and conditions of the owner. Do not make illegal copies of books or software. If you believe that this book, related materials, or any other Element K materials are being reproduced or transmitted without permission, please call (800) 478-7788.

Element K is independent from Microsoft Corporation, and is not affiliated with Microsoft in any manner. While this publication and CD-ROM may be used in assisting individuals to prepare for a Microsoft Business Certification exam, Microsoft, its designated program administrator, and Element K do not warrant that use of this publication and CD-ROM will ensure passing a Microsoft Business Certification exam.

What is the Microsoft Business Certification Program?

The Microsoft Business Certification Program enables candidates to show that they have something exceptional to offer – proven expertise in Microsoft Office programs. The two certification tracks allow candidates to choose how they want to exhibit their skills, either through validating skills within a specific Microsoft product or taking their knowledge to the next level and combining Microsoft programs to show that they can apply multiple skill sets to complete more complex office tasks. Recognized by businesses and schools around the world, over 3 million certifications have been obtained in over 100 different countries. The Microsoft Business Certification Program is the only Microsoft-approved certification program of its kind.

What is the Microsoft Certified Application Specialist Certification?

The Microsoft Certified Application Specialist Certification exams focus on validating specific skill sets within each of the Microsoft® Office system programs. The candidate can choose which exam(s) they want to take according to which skills they want to validate. The available Application Specialist exams include:

- Using Microsoft® Windows Vista™
- Using Microsoft® Office Word 2007
- Using Microsoft® Office Excel® 2007
- Using Microsoft® Office PowerPoint® 2007
- Using Microsoft® Office Access 2007
- Using Microsoft® Office Outlook® 2007

What is the Microsoft Certified Application Professional Certification?

The Microsoft Certified Application Professional Certification exams focus on a candidate's ability to use the 2007 Microsoft® Office system to accomplish industry-agnostic functions, for example Budget Analysis and Forecasting, or Content Management and Collaboration. The available Application Professional exams currently include:

- Organizational Support
- Creating and Managing Presentations
- Content Management and Collaboration
- Budget Analysis and Forecasting

What do the Microsoft Business Certification Vendor of Approved Courseware logos represent?

The logos validate that the courseware has been approved by the Microsoft® Business Certification Vendor program and that these courses cover objectives that will be included in the relevant exam. It also means that after utilizing this courseware, you may be prepared to pass the exams required to become a Microsoft Certified Application Specialist or Microsoft Certified Application Professional.

For more information:

To learn more about Microsoft Certified Application Specialist or Professional exams, visit **www.microsoft.com/learning/msbc**.

To learn about other Microsoft Certified Application Specialist approved courseware from Element K, visit **www.elementkcourseware.com**.

* The availability of Microsoft Certified Application exams varies by Microsoft Office program, program version and language. Visit **www.microsoft.com/learning** for exam availability.

Microsoft, the Office Logo, Outlook, and PowerPoint are either registered trademarks or trademarks of Microsoft Corporation in the United States and/or other countries. The Microsoft Certified Application Specialist and Microsoft Certified Application Professional Logos are used under license from Microsoft Corporation.

Microsoft® Office Access™ 2007: Level 1 (Second Edition)

About This Course

Most organizations maintain and manage large amounts of information. One of the most efficient and powerful ways of managing data is by using relational databases. Information can be stored, linked, and managed using a single relational database application and its associated tools. In this course, you will examine the basic database concepts, and create and modify databases and their various objects using the Microsoft® Office Access™ 2007 relational database application.

Managing large amounts of complex information is common in today's business environment and, if done properly, can provide any business an edge over the competition. However, mismanaged and lost information can cause you to fall behind. Managing data using the Access 2007 database application can give your business that positive edge.

This course can also benefit you if you are preparing to take the Microsoft Certified Application Specialist exam for Microsoft® Access™ 2007. Please refer to the CD-ROM that came with this course for a document that maps exam objectives to the content in the Microsoft Office Access Courseware series. To access the mapping document, insert the CD-ROM into your CD-ROM drive and at the root of the ROM, double-click ExamMapping.doc to open the mapping document.

If your book did not come with a CD, please go to **http:// www.elementk.com/ courseware-file-downloads** to download the data files.

In addition to the mapping document, two assessment files per course can be found on the CD-ROM to check your knowledge. To access the assessments, at the root of the course part number folder, double-click 084887s3.doc to view the assessments without the answers marked, or double-click 084887ie.doc to view the assessments with the answers marked.

Course Description

Target Student

This course is designed for students who wish to learn the basic operations of the Microsoft Access database application to perform their day-to-day responsibilities, and to understand the advantages that using a relational database application can bring to their business processes. The Level 1 course is for the individual whose job responsibilities include designing and creating new databases, tables, and relationships; creating and maintaining records; locating records; and producing reports based on the information in the database. Individuals who want to pursue Microsoft Certified Application Specialist certification in Microsoft Office Access 2007 can also take this course.

Course Prerequisites

Students should have completed the following courses or possess equivalent knowledge before starting this course:

- *Windows 2000: Introduction*
- *Windows XP: Introduction*
- *Windows XP: Level 1*
- *Windows XP: Level 2*

How to Use This Book

As a Learning Guide

Each lesson covers one broad topic or set of related topics. Lessons are arranged in order of increasing proficiency with *Microsoft® Office Access 2007*; skills you acquire in one lesson are used and developed in subsequent lessons. For this reason, you should work through the lessons in sequence.

We organized each lesson into results-oriented topics. Topics include all the relevant and supporting information you need to master *Microsoft® Office Access 2007*, and activities allow you to apply this information to practical hands-on examples.

You get to try out each new skill on a specially prepared sample file. This saves you typing time and allows you to concentrate on the skill at hand. Through the use of sample files, hands-on activities, illustrations that give you feedback at crucial steps, and supporting background information, this book provides you with the foundation and structure to learn *Microsoft® Office Access 2007* quickly and easily.

As a Review Tool

Any method of instruction is only as effective as the time and effort you are willing to invest in it. In addition, some of the information that you learn in class may not be important to you immediately, but it may become important later on. For this reason, we encourage you to spend some time reviewing the topics and activities after the course. For an additional challenge when reviewing activities, try the "What You Do" column before looking at the "How You Do It" column.

As a Reference

The organization and layout of the book make it easy to use as a learning tool and as an after-class reference. You can use this book as a first source for definitions of terms, background information on given topics, and summaries of procedures.

Course Icons

Icon	Description
	A **Caution Note** makes students aware of potential negative consequences of an action, setting, or decision that are not easily known.
	Display Slide provides a prompt to the instructor to display a specific slide. Display Slides are included in the Instructor Guide only.
	An **Instructor Note** is a comment to the instructor regarding delivery, classroom strategy, classroom tools, exceptions, and other special considerations. Instructor Notes are included in the Instructor Guide only.
	Notes Page indicates a page that has been left intentionally blank for students to write on.
	A **Student Note** provides additional information, guidance, or hints about a topic or task.
	A **Version Note** indicates information necessary for a specific version of software.

Certification

This course is designed to help you prepare for the following certification.

Certification Path: Microsoft Certified Application Specialist – Access™ 2007

This course is one of a series of Element K courseware titles that addresses Microsoft Certified Application Specialist (Microsoft Business Certification) skill sets. The Microsoft Certified Application Specialist program is for individuals who use Microsoft's business desktop software and who seek recognition for their expertise with specific Microsoft products. Certification candidates must pass one or more proficiency exams in order to earn Microsoft Certified Application Specialist certification.

Common Jkkmvop

Course Objectives

In this course, you will create and modify new databases and their various objects.

You will:

- examine the basic database concepts and explore the Microsoft Office Access 2007 environment.
- design a simple database.
- build a new database with related tables.
- manage data in a table.
- query a database using different methods.
- design forms.
- generate reports.

Course Requirements

Hardware

For this course, you will need one computer for each student and one for the instructor. Each computer will need the following minimum hardware components:

- A 1 GHz Pentium-class processor or faster.
- A minimum of 256 MB of RAM. 512 MB of RAM is recommended.
- A 10 GB hard disk or larger. You should have at least 1 GB of free hard disk space available for the Office installation.
- A CD-ROM drive.
- A keyboard and mouse or other pointing device.
- A 1024 x 768 resolution monitor is recommended.
- Network cards and cabling for local network access.
- Internet access (see your local network administrator).
- A printer (optional) or an installed printer driver.
- A projection system to display the instructor's computer screen.

Software

- Microsoft® Office Professional Edition 2007.
- Microsoft Office Suite Service Pack 1.
- Windows XP Professional with Service Pack 2.

  This course was developed using the Windows XP operating system; however, the manufacturer's documentation states that it will also run on Vista. If you use Vista, you might notice some slight differences when keying the course.

Class Setup

Initial Class Setup

For initial class setup:

1. Install Windows XP Professional on an empty partition.

    ■   Leave the Administrator password blank.

    ■   For all other installation parameters, use values that are appropriate for your environment (see your local network administrator for details).

2. On Windows XP Professional, disable the Welcome screen. (This step ensures that students will be able to log on as the Administrator user regardless of what other user accounts exist on the computer.)

    a. Click Start and choose Control Panel→User Accounts.

    b. Click Change The Way Users Log On And Off.

    c. Uncheck Use Welcome Screen.

    d. Click Apply Options.

3. On XP Professional, install Service Pack 2. Use the Service Pack installation defaults.

4. On the computer, install a printer driver (a physical print device is optional). Click Start and choose Printers And Faxes. Under Printer Tasks, click Add A Printer and follow the prompts.

    If you do not have a physical printer installed, right-click the printer and choose Pause Printing to prevent any print error messages.

5. Run the Internet Connection Wizard to set up the Internet connection as appropriate for your environment if you did not do so during installation.

6. Display known file type extensions.

    a. Open Windows Explorer (right-click Start and select Explore).

    b. Choose Tools→Folder Options.

    c. On the View tab, in the Advanced Settings list box, uncheck Hide Extensions For Known File Types.

    d. Click Apply and then click OK.

    e. Close Windows Explorer.

7. Log on to the computer as the Administrator user if you have not already done so.

8. Perform a Complete installation of Microsoft Office Professional 2007.

9. In the User Name dialog box, click OK to accept the default user name and initials.

10. In the Microsoft Office 2007 Activation Wizard dialog box, click Next to activate the Office 2007 application.

11. When the activation of Microsoft Office 2007 is complete, click Close to close the Microsoft Office 2007 Activation Wizard dialog box.

12. In the User Name dialog box, click OK.

13. In the Welcome To Microsoft 2007! dialog box, click Finish. You must have an active Internet connection in order to complete this step. Here, you select the Download And Install Updates From Microsoft Update When Available (Recommended) option, so that whenever there is a new update, it gets automatically installed in your system.

14. After the Microsoft Update runs, in the Microsoft Office dialog box, click OK.

15. If necessary, minimize the Language Bar.

16. On the course CD-ROM, open the 084_887 folder. Then, open the Data folder. Run the 084887dd.exe self-extracting file located in it. This will install a folder named 084887Data on your C drive. This folder contains all the data files that you will use to complete this course.

Within each lesson folder, you may find a Solution folder. This folder contains solution files for the lesson's activities and lesson lab, which can be used by students to check their end results.

If your book did not come with a CD, please go to **http://www.elementk.com/courseware-file-downloads** to download the data files.

Customize the Windows Desktop

Customize the Windows desktop to display the My Computer and My Network Places icons on the student and instructor systems by following these steps:

1. Right-click the Desktop and choose Properties.

2. Select the Desktop tab.

3. Click Customize Desktop.

4. In the Desktop Items dialog box, check My Computer and My Network Places.

5. Click OK and click Apply.

6. Close the Display Properties dialog box.

Configure Trust Center Settings

1. From the Office Button menu, click Access Options.

2. Select the Trust Center category.

3. Click Trust Center Settings.

4. In the Trust Center dialog box, select the Macro Settings category and select the Disable All Macros Except Digitally Signed Macros option.

5. In the Trust Center dialog box, select the Trusted Locations category and click Add New Location.

6. In the Microsoft Office Trusted Location dialog box, click Browse and navigate to the C:\084887Data folder and click OK.

7. In the Microsoft Office Trusted Location dialog box, check the Subfolders Of This Location Are Also Trusted check box.

8. Click OK.

9. Click OK to close the Trust Center dialog box.

10. Click OK to close the Access Options dialog box.

Configuring Add-Ins

Find add-ins for other file formats.

1. In the left pane under Template Categories, select the Featuring category.

2. In the Microsoft Office Online box, under More On Office Online, click the Downloads link.

3. In the Downloads text box, type Microsoft save as PDF or XPS add-in for 2007 Microsoft Office programs and click Search.

4. Click the 2007 Microsoft Office Add-in: Microsoft Save As PDF Or XPS link.

5. In the Quick Details section, from the Estimated Download Time drop-down list, select the appropriate network connection type.

6. Verify that the language is set to English, and then click Continue next to Validation Required.

7. Follow the instructions to download and install the add-in.

8. Close the browser window.

9. Click the Office button and click Exit Access to close the application.

Before Every Class

1. Log on to the computer as the Administrator user.

2. Delete any existing data files from the C:\084887Data folder.

3. Extract a fresh copy of the course data files from the CD-ROM provided with the course manual.

List of Additional Files

Printed with each activity is a list of files students open to complete that activity. Many activities also require additional files that students do not open, but are needed to support the file(s) students are working with. These supporting files are included with the student data files on the course CD-ROM or data disk. Do not delete these files.

1 | Exploring the Microsoft® Office Access™ 2007 Environment

Lesson Time: 50 minutes

Lesson Objectives:

In this lesson, you will examine the basic database concepts and explore the Microsoft Office Access 2007 environment.

You will:

- Examine database concepts.
- Explore the user interface of Microsoft Access 2007.
- Use an existing Access database.
- Customize the Access environment.
- Obtain help using the Access 2007 Help feature.

Introduction

In most businesses, working with large amounts of varying types of data is a daily requirement. Understanding the concepts of databases and their components will provide you with a foundation for using Microsoft® Office Access™ 2007 to organize your data. In this lesson, you will examine basic database concepts and explore the Access 2007 environment.

Imagine using a computer without having a basic understanding of its components and how it operates! You need to get familiar with the components of a database application such as Access before you work with it. This will make your job less tedious. Exploring the Access environment will introduce you to some of its basic tools and functions, which will help you get started with Access.

TOPIC A
Examine Database Concepts

If you work with large amounts of data, you know that it is important to logically group data and store it for future use. A database is a useful tool for organizing, storing, and retrieving data efficiently. If you have never used a database, understanding what a database is and knowing the terms used to describe a database are the first steps to becoming a competent database user. In this topic, you will be introduced to database concepts.

Working with databases has become inevitable in any business environment. Familiarizing yourself with the basic concepts of a database will help you work with them easily.

Databases

Definition:

A *database* is a collection of data that is logically related and organized so that a computer program can access the desired information quickly. The data contained in a database can be textual, numeric, or graphical. The data in the database can be searched, retrieved, and manipulated.

Example:

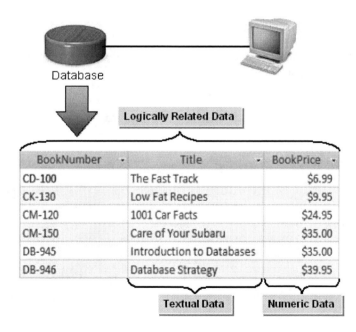

Figure 1-1: *A database.*

Database Terminology

Like many other computer programs, database applications have their own terminology to refer to the various components of a database.

Term	Description
Table	A group of records stored in rows and columns.
Record	A set of data pertaining to one person or entity.
Field	A category of information that pertains to all records.
Value	A single piece of data.

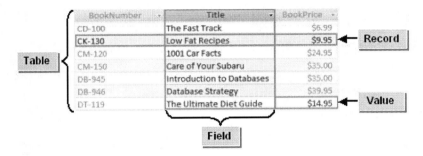

Figure 1-2: Components of a database.

Relational Databases

Definition:

Relational databases are databases that store information in multiple tables that are interrelated. Each table stores one specific category of information. Relational databases can access these tables and extract, reorganize, and display the information contained within them in many different ways without altering the structure of the original tables.

Example:

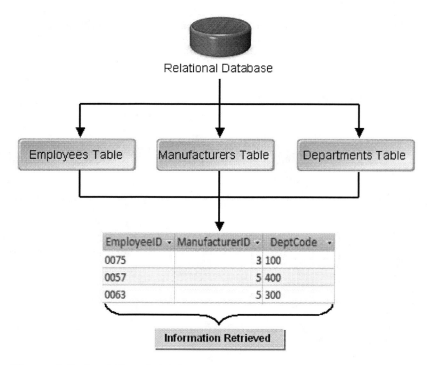

Figure 1-3: A relational database.

ACTIVITY 1-1
Examining Database Concepts

Scenario:
You have started working as a customer relations executive in a travel agency. The agency stores all its customer and travel information in a database. As you interact with customers, you may need to use the database for storing and retrieving data. Before starting off with your work, you want to make sure that you understand the basic concepts of databases and the terminology used to refer to their various components.

1. **Which term is used to refer to a single piece of data?**

   a) Table

   b) Field

   c) Value

   d) Record

2. **What does the term record refer to?**

   a) Set of data pertaining to one person or entity

   b) Single piece of data

   c) Category of information that pertains to all records

   d) Group of records stored in rows and columns

TOPIC B
Explore the User Interface

Having examined the concepts of databases and their components, you are now ready to work with a database application. Microsoft Office Access 2007 is a robust and easy-to-use application that even beginners can learn quickly. In order to start working with Access 2007, you first need to be familiar with the various elements of its interface. In this topic, you will explore the user interface of Access 2007.

Starting to work with a software application without having explored its environment is much like entering a house without knowing how to open any of the doors to the rooms. Working with Access can become easier if you first understand the utilities of the various elements of its interface. Also, while managing or creating a database, you will not waste time searching for commands if you are sure about their locations.

Microsoft Office Access 2007

Microsoft Office Access 2007 is a database application used for creating and managing databases. By using this application, you can quickly retrieve the desired information from a database and also update it. It provides you with various features for creating and editing tables, forms, and reports. You can display sorted, filtered, and grouped data. Additionally, Access 2007 allows you to import and export data from external applications and from the web.

The Getting Started With Microsoft Office Access Window

The *Getting Started With Microsoft Office Access window* is the first window that appears when you start Access 2007. Using this window, you can choose either a blank database, or one of the ready-to-use database templates, through which you can start working on databases without much effort. There are many template categories available, such as Education and Business. From this window, you can also connect to Microsoft Office online for finding help and downloading templates across various categories. The templates can be customized to suit your requirements. You can also access recently opened databases from the right pane of the window.

The Access Application Window

When you create a new database or open an existing database, the Access application window is displayed. The Access application window consists of various interface elements to assist you while you are working on a database.

Window Element	Description
The Office button	A standard button that displays a menu containing various functions to open, save, print, and close an Access database.
The Quick Access toolbar	A toolbar that provides easy access to frequently used commands in the application.

Window Element	Description
The Ribbon	A panel that contains task-specific commands grouped under different command tabs.
The Navigation Pane	A pane that displays the database objects such as tables, queries, forms, and reports.
The Microsoft Office status bar	A window element that enables you to switch between different views in which the database objects can be viewed.
Dialog Box Launcher	Are miniature buttons that accompany groups on the command tabs. When you click a button, a dialog box that provides additional commands and tools associated with the group is launched.

Figure 1-4: *The Access interface elements.*

The Office Button

The *Office button* is a standard button that is located in the top-left corner of the Access window and is part of most Microsoft Office 2007 applications. When you click this button, a menu is displayed that provides a set of commands for creating a new database, and for opening, saving, printing, managing, emailing, publishing, and closing a database. The menu also has the Access Options button that you can use to customize the Access environment. Further, a list of recently opened databases is retained in the Office button menu enabling you to quickly access the databases you have been working on.

The Quick Access Toolbar

The *Quick Access toolbar* is a toolbar that holds frequently used commands such as Save, Undo, and Redo, and is located above the Ribbon as an integrated component of the title bar. The commands on the Quick Access toolbar are available regardless of which command tab you select on the Ribbon. You can, however, customize the Quick Access toolbar to include additional commands that you frequently use. You can also place the Quick Access toolbar below the Ribbon.

The Ribbon

The *Ribbon* is a new interface component that contains task-specific commands grouped together under different command tabs. It has been designed to be the primary location for accessing various commands. The Ribbon enables you to easily identify the desired tools or functions, and perform both simple and advanced operations without having to navigate extensively.

ScreenTip

A *ScreenTip* is a label that appears when you place the mouse pointer over a command or control in the interface. It contains a description of the task performed by the control or command. This feature has been incorporated for most of the common options that you may work with. However, the ScreenTip for other options and command buttons provides only the name of the component.

Command Tabs

The following table lists the command tabs on the Ribbon in Access.

Command Tab	Contains Commands For
Home	Organizing and manipulating data present in the database objects.
Create	Creating database objects.
External Data	Importing and exporting data.
Database Tools	Manipulating macros, defining relationships, showing or hiding specific tools, analyzing data, moving data to a server, and accessing database tools.

Contextual Tabs

Contextual tabs are tabs with specialized commands that are displayed on the Ribbon when you select an object such as a table, form, or report. They are displayed along with the core tabs that exist by default on the Ribbon, and you can use them to modify and format the selected object. You can switch between the contextual tabs and the core tabs as needed. However, when you deselect the object, the contextual tabs disappear.

The Navigation Pane

The *Navigation Pane* is located on the left side of the Access window and displays database objects such as tables, forms, queries, and reports. Using the Navigation Pane, you can navigate between database objects. You can also customize the Navigation Pane to display the navigation items to suit your requirements.

The Tabbed Document Window Viewing Feature

The *Tabbed Document Window Viewing* feature displays the open database objects such as tables, queries, and forms as tabs in the same window. This feature enables you to easily navigate between the objects.

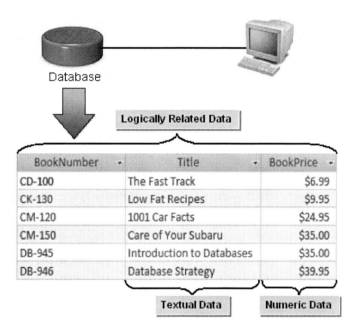

Figure 1-5: *The Tabbed Document Window Viewing feature.*

The Microsoft Office Status Bar

The *Microsoft Office status bar* is located at the bottom of the application window and offers additional convenient features. Using the Microsoft Office status bar, you can switch between different views in which the database objects can be viewed. By right-clicking the Microsoft Office status bar, you can set options such as Caps Lock, Scroll Lock, or Num Lock.

Galleries

A *gallery* is a repository for elements of the same category and acts as a central location for accessing the various styles and appearance settings for an object. Galleries provide you with a set of visual choices to enhance the look and feel of database elements while working on a database.

ACTIVITY 1-2

Exploring the User Interface

Data Files:

Books.accdb

Scenario:

Your company has just purchased and installed the Microsoft Office 2007 package. As you will be working with Access frequently, you decide to spend some time exploring the new user interface elements of the Access environment.

What You Do	How You Do It
1. Explore the Getting Started With Microsoft Access window.	a. **Choose Start→All Programs→Microsoft Office→Microsoft Office Access 2007** to launch the Microsoft Office Access 2007 application.
	b. In the left pane, in the From Microsoft Office Online section, **click a category.**
	c. Observe that the middle pane displays the templates available in the selected category.
2. Explore the Office button menu.	a. **Click the Office button.** 🔘
	b. Notice that the menu displays the options for creating, saving, printing, managing, emailing, publishing, and closing the database.
	c. **Click outside the menu** to close it.
3. Open an existing database using the Office button.	a. **Click the Office button and choose Open.**
	b. In the Open dialog box, **navigate to the C:\084887Data\Exploring the Access Environment folder.**
	c. In the Open dialog box, **select Books.accdb and click Open.**
	d. In the Navigation Pane, **double-click tblBookOrders** to open the tblBookOrders table.

4.	**Explore the Quick Access toolbar.**	a.	On the Quick Access toolbar, **place the mouse pointer over each button** to view the ScreenTip.
		b.	**Click the Customize Quick Access Toolbar drop-down arrow** to view the options.
		c.	**Click anywhere outside the drop-down list** to close it.
5.	**Explore the Ribbon.**	a.	Observe the various groups of commands on the Home tab such as Views, Clipboard, Font, Rich Text, Records, Sort & Filter, and Find.
		b.	On the Ribbon, **select a tab** to view the commands.
		c.	Observe the various commands and buttons that perform functions specific to the selected tab.
6.	**Explore the Microsoft Office status bar.**	a.	In the lower-right corner, on the Microsoft Office status bar, **position the mouse pointer over each button** to view the ScreenTip.
		b.	**Right-click the Microsoft Office status bar and view the options.**
		c.	**Click anywhere outside the menu** to close it.
7.	**Explore the Navigation Pane.**	a.	In the Navigation Pane, **click the Shutter Bar Open/Close button** [«] to collapse the Navigation Pane.
		b.	At the top of the Navigation Pane, **click the Shutter Bar Open/Close button** to expand the Navigation Pane.

c. **Place the mouse pointer on the separator line between the Navigation Pane and the Tabbed Document.** When the pointer changes to a double-headed arrow, **click and drag the mouse pointer approximately one inch to the left** to decrease the size of the Navigation Pane.

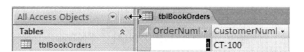

8.	**Explore using the Dialog Box Launcher button on the Home tab.**	a.	On the Ribbon, **select the Home tab.**
		b.	At the bottom-right corner of the Font group, **click the Dialog Box Launcher button.** ⌞⊠⌟
		c.	Observe that the Datasheet Formatting dialog box is displayed.
		d.	In the Datasheet Formatting dialog box, **click the Close button** to close the dialog box.

9.	**Display the Font Color gallery.**	a.	In the Font group, **click the Font Color drop-down arrow** ⌞A ▾⌟to display the Font color gallery.
		b.	**At the top right of the Tabbed Document window, click the Close button to close the tblBookOrders table.**

TOPIC C
Use an Existing Access Database

In the previous topic, you explored the various interface components of the Access application. Before designing and creating your own database, you want to explore an existing database and its various objects. In this topic, you will use an existing Access database.

In order to effectively design and create your own databases in Access 2007, it is important to have first used the application and some existing databases. Compared with spreadsheets or word processing applications, a database application, such as Access, is a little more complicated. Having experience with the objects available in an existing database will enable you to make the right decision in designing and creating your own databases.

Tables

Definition:

A *table* is a collection of related information arranged in rows and columns. Information about each item in the collection is displayed as a row. The columns contain the same category of information for every item in the table. A table has a header row that identifies the category of information in each column.

Example:

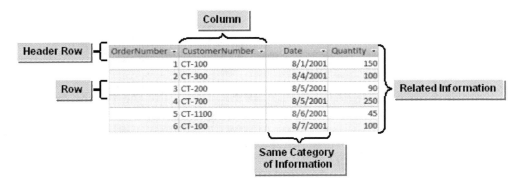

Figure 1-6: A table.

Queries

Definition:

A *query* is an instruction that requests information from the tables present in a database. A query requires the field and table names to generate the output. It can include conditions to retrieve specific information. Queries can be saved for reuse. Apart from retrieving data from specific fields of tables, queries can also perform calculations and display the results.

Example:

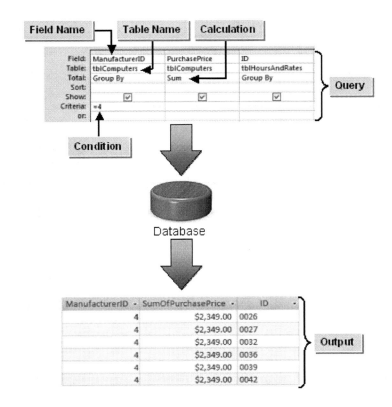

Figure 1-7: A query.

Recordsets

Definition:

A *recordset* is a table that displays groups of records either from a base table or as the result of an executed query. The data displayed in a recordset is physically located within a larger source, such as a table.

Example:

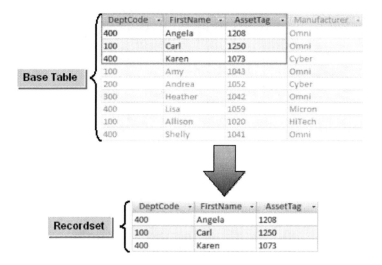

Figure 1-8: A recordset from a base table.

Forms

Definition:

A *form* is a graphical interface that is used to display and edit data. Forms can be based on a table or a query. Data is never stored in forms; a form only displays the data stored in a table. Forms can be customized according to the viewing needs of the user. In addition to displaying table data, forms can include calculations, graphics, and other objects.

Example:

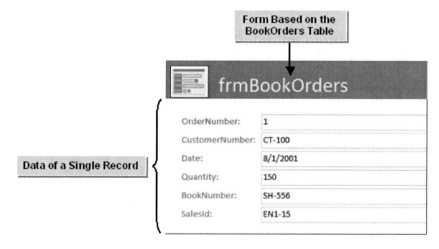

Figure 1-9: A form.

Reports

Definition:

A *report* is a screen output of data arranged in an order specified by the user. It consists of information retrieved from tables or queries. Reports can also perform calculations and display the results. Reports are often created for the purpose of printing data.

Example:

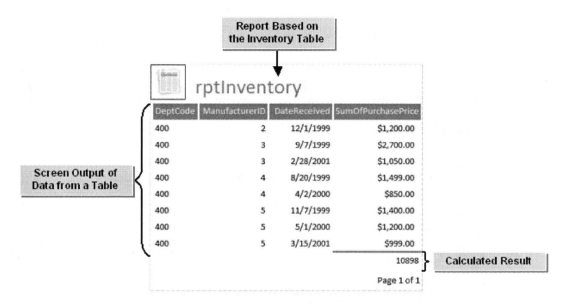

Figure 1-10: A report.

Naming Conventions in Access

Naming conventions in Access are widely accepted guidelines for naming database objects in order to identify them easily. The guidelines call for a unique prefix to be assigned to an object name. Naming conventions are optional and the type of naming convention utilized is strictly based on the discretion of the user.

Object	Prefix	Example
Table	tbl	tblSampleTable
Select Queries	qry	qrySampleQuery
Form	frm	frmSampleForm
Subform	fsub	fsubSampleSubform
Report	rpt	rptSampleReport
Subreport	rsub	rsubSampleSubReport

How to Use an Existing Access Database

Procedure Reference: View Data in a Table

To view data in a table:

1. If necessary, click the Navigation Pane drop-down arrow and select Tables to display the list of tables in the database.
2. Open the desired table to view data contained in it.
   - In the Navigation Pane, right-click the desired table and choose Open.
   - Or, double-click the desired table.
3. If necessary, close the table.
   - Right-click the table document tab and choose Close.
   - Or, at the top-right corner of the Tabbed Document window, click the Close button.

Procedure Reference: Run a Query

To run a query:

1. If necessary, click the Navigation Pane drop-down arrow and select Queries to display the list of existing queries in the database.
2. Run the desired query.
   - In the Navigation Pane, right-click the desired query and choose Open.
   - Or, double-click the desired query.
3. If necessary, close the query.
   - Right-click the query document tab and choose Close.
   - Or, at the top-right corner of the Tabbed Document window, click the Close button.

Procedure Reference: View Data Using a Form

To view data using a form:

1. If necessary, click the Navigation Pane drop-down arrow and select Forms to display the list of existing forms in the database.
2. Open the desired form to view data contained in the table, record by record.
3. If necessary, close the form.

Procedure Reference: View a Report

To view the data in a report:

1. Click the Navigation Pane drop-down arrow and select Reports to display the list of reports in the database.
2. Open the desired report to view the print format of data.
3. If necessary, close the report.

ACTIVITY 1-3

Using an Existing Access Database

Data Files:

Books.accdb

Before You Begin:

From the C:\084887Data\Exploring the Access Environment folder, open the Books.accdb file.

Scenario:

You have been asked to retrieve certain data from a database and update it. Also, you want to prepare a hard copy of the updated data. However, you are still unsure about how to use the various database objects to get your job done.

What You Do	How You Do It
1. **View the data in a table.**	a. In the Navigation Pane, **right-click tblBooks and choose Open** to open the table.
	b. Observe that the data is stored in three different fields in the table.
	c. **Right-click the tblBooks document tab and choose Close** to close the table.

2. Run a query.

a. **Click the Navigation Pane drop-down arrow and select Queries.**

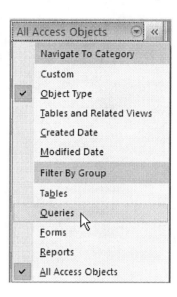

b. In the Navigation Pane, observe that the list of existing queries in the database is displayed.

c. In the Navigation Pane, **double-click qryBookOrders** to run the query.

d. Observe that the query displays only the CustomerNumber, BookNumber, and the SalesId fields.

e. At the top-right corner of the Tabbed Document window, **click the Close button** to close the query.

3. **View a form.**

    a. **Click the Navigation Pane drop-down arrow and select Forms.**

    b. In the Navigation Pane, observe that the list of existing forms in the database is displayed.

    c. In the Navigation Pane, **right-click frmBookOrders and choose Open** to open the form.

    d. Observe that all data pertaining to the first record of the table is displayed in the form.

    e. **Right-click the FrmBookOrders document tab and choose Close** to close the form.

4. **View a report.**

    a. **Click the Navigation Pane drop-down arrow and select Reports.**

    b. In the Navigation Pane, observe that the list of existing reports in the database is displayed.

    c. In the Navigation Pane, **double-click rptBooks** to open the report.

    d. Observe that the print format of the data is displayed in the report.

    e. At the top-right corner of the document window, **click the Close button** to close the report.

    f. **Click the Navigation Pane drop-down arrow and select All Access Objects.**

    g. **Verify that all the tables, queries, forms, and reports are now all visible at one time.**

TOPIC D
Customize the Access Environment

Having worked with the various objects of an existing database, you can now manipulate the database to suit your needs. Before you begin, you may want to alter the default settings of the interface elements to suit your workflow and preferences. In this topic, you will customize the Access environment.

When you work with a software application, you may have to use certain tools and commands more frequently. Making those tools and commands quickly accessible will help you work efficiently. In Access 2007, it is possible to customize the user interface and its elements to suit your work requirements.

The Access Options Dialog Box

The Access Options dialog box provides you with various categories of options to customize the Access environment. You can use the various options under different categories to change the default settings of the various database objects. The Trust Center category contains options for security and privacy, which you can customize according to your requirements. You can also customize the Quick Access toolbar using the options in the Customize category.

How to Customize the Access Environment

Procedure Reference: Customize the Access Environment Using the Access Options Dialog Box

To customize the Access Environment using the Access Options dialog box:

1. Click the Office button and then click Access Options.
2. In the Access Options dialog box, in the left pane, select the desired category.
3. In the Access Options dialog box, in the right pane, select the desired commands.
4. Click OK to apply the changes.

Procedure Reference: Customize the Quick Access Toolbar

To customize the Quick Access toolbar:

1. If desired, on the Quick Access toolbar, click the Customize Quick Access Toolbar drop-down arrow and select Show Before The Ribbon to place the Quick Access toolbar below the Ribbon.

> To place the Quick Access toolbar below the Ribbon, you can also display the Customize category in the Access Options dialog box and check the Show Quick Access Toolbar Below The Ribbon check box.

2. Display the Customize category in the Access Options dialog box.
    *   On the Quick Access toolbar, click the Customize Quick Access Toolbar drop-down arrow and select More Commands.
    *   Or, click the Office button, click Access Options, and then select the Customize category.

3. Customize the Quick Access toolbar.

    a. In the Access Options dialog box, in the right pane, from the Choose Commands From drop-down list, select an option.

    b. From the Customize Quick Access Toolbar drop-down list, select an option for specifying that the changes need to be applied to all databases or to the active database only.

    c. Customize commands on the Quick Access toolbar.

        ●   In the Choose Commands From section, in the list box, select a command and click Add to add the command to the Quick Access toolbar.

        ●   In the Customize Quick Access Toolbar section, in the list box, select a command and click Remove to remove the command from the Quick Access toolbar.

    d. Position items on the Quick Access toolbar.

        ●   In the Customize Quick Access Toolbar section, in the list box, select a command and click the Move Up button to move the item up in the list.

        ●   In the Customize Quick Access Toolbar section, in the list box, select a command and click the Move Down button to move the item down in the list.

4. In the Access Options dialog box, click OK to apply the changes.

Procedure Reference: Customize the Microsoft Office Status Bar

To customize the Microsoft Office status bar:

1. Right-click the Microsoft Office status bar to display the context menu.

2. On the context menu, select or deselect an option for adding or removing it from the Microsoft Office status bar.

ACTIVITY 1-4
Customizing the Access Environment

Before You Begin:
The Books.accdb file is open.

Scenario:
You are familiar with the Access environment and are set to begin work. However, before you start working on your project, you would like to make some changes to the interface so that you can access commands and options in order to suit your needs. You would also like to change the default appearance of the datasheet.

What You Do	How You Do It
1. Customize the appearance of datasheets using the Access Options dialog box.	a. **Click the Office button and then click Access Options.**
	b. In the Access Options dialog box, in the left pane, **select Datasheet.**
	c. In the right pane, in the Default Colors section, **click the Font Color button,** and in the Standard Colors section, in the first row, in the sixth column, **select Maroon.**

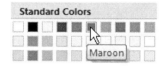

	d. **Click the Background Color button,** and in the Standard Colors section, in the fourth row, in the seventh column, **select Green 3.**
	e. In the Access Options dialog box, **click OK.**
	f. In the Navigation Pane, **double-click tblCustomers** to open the table.
	g. Observe that the datasheet displays the colors that were selected.

2. **Customize the Quick Access toolbar.**

    a. On the Quick Access toolbar, **click the Customize Quick Access Toolbar drop-down arrow and select More Commands.**

    b. In the Access Options dialog box, from the Choose Commands From drop-down list, **select All Commands.**

    c. In the list box below the Choose Commands From drop-down list, **scroll down and select Close Database.**

    d. **Click Add.**

    e. In the Choose Commands From section, in the list box, **scroll down and select Open.**

    f. **Click Add.**

    g. In the Access Options dialog box, **click OK.**

    h. On the Quick Access toolbar, observe that the added options are displayed.

3. **Customize the Microsoft Office status bar.**

    a. **Right-click the Microsoft Office status bar and deselect View Shortcuts.**

    b. **Click away from the menu** to close it.

    c. Observe that the shortcut buttons are removed from the Microsoft Office status bar.

    d. **Right-click the Microsoft Office status bar and select View Shortcuts.**

    e. On the Quick Access toolbar, **click the Close Database button** to close the database.

TOPIC E
Obtain Help

Having customized the Access environment to suit your work requirements, you can now begin working with Access. As you work, you may come across tools and options that are unfamiliar to you and might need some help in discovering how to use them. In this topic, you will obtain help using the Access 2007 Help feature.

When testing new equipment, you would refer to the product manual and catalog to learn about the various features and functionality. Similarly, as a new user using the Access application, you may want to try out some new tasks. The Access 2007 Help feature provides you with comprehensive offline and online links to answer your questions.

Access 2007 Help

The *Access Help* feature is a complete user manual on the functionality of the various features of Microsoft Access 2007. The Access Help window provides a quick and easy way to find answers to Access-related queries, online or offline.

Window Element	Allows You To
Access Help toolbar	Access commands for navigating through the various Help topics.
Type Words To Search For text box	Search for information on any topic in Access by specifying a query.
Search drop-down list	Specify that the search has to be performed online or offline.
Browse Access Help pane	Browse through various Help topics organized under different categories.
Table Of Contents pane	Access the Table Of Contents for all Access Help topics.

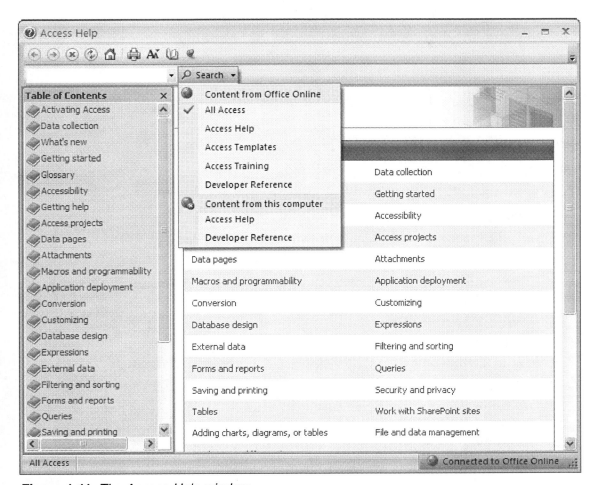

Figure 1-11: The Access Help window.

Areas of Search in Access Help

You can specify a search area to narrow down the search results to that specific area. You can either use the Help feature within the application or select an option from the Content From Office Online section to search the web for help on the desired topic.

Area of Search	Description
All Access	Lists information on the query from the built-in Help feature and provides help links from the Microsoft Office website, if required.
Access Help	Lists information on the query from the built-in Help feature as well as the Microsoft Office website, but does not take you to the Office website.
Access Templates	Lists sample templates that are available from the Microsoft Office website.
Access Training	Lists sample training information links from the Microsoft Office website.

Area of Search	Description
Developer Reference	Lists programming tasks, samples, and references to guide you in developing customized solutions based on Access.

How to Obtain Help

Procedure Reference: Obtain Help

To find information in Access Help:

1. Open the Access Help window.

   - On the Ribbon, click the Microsoft Office Access Help button.
   - Or, press F1.

2. If desired, on the Access Help toolbar, click the Show Table Of Contents button to display the Table Of Contents pane.

3. Click a link to view its details.

   - In the Table Of Contents pane, click a link to view its details.
   - Or, in the Browse Access Help pane, click a link to view its details.

4. If desired, search for information.

   a. To narrow the search to a particular area, select an option from the Search drop-down list.

   b. In the Type Words To Search For text box, type a keyword.

   c. Click Search to display the search results.

5. If desired, at the top-right corner of the Access Help window, click the Close button to close the window.

Keeping the Access Help Window on Top

You can set the Access Help window so that it stays on top of the Access window or other Microsoft Office windows. To determine the current mode, point to the Not On Top/Keep On Top button. The ScreenTip should tell you the mode the Help window is in. To toggle to the other mode, click the button.

ACTIVITY 1-5

Obtaining Help

Before You Begin:
Launch the Access 2007 application.

Scenario:
You need to create a new table in your company's employee information database and generate a report based on that table. Being a first-time user, you are not very clear on how to proceed with this job. You think it would be helpful if you can obtain some additional information on the various methods and commands used to create a table and a report.

What You Do	How You Do It
1. View the content of a Help topic.	a. At the top-right corner of the Access application, **click the Microsoft Office Access Help button.**
	b. At the top-right corner of the Access Help window, **click the Maximize button** to maximize the window.
	c. In the Browse Access Help pane, **click the Tables link.**
	d. Observe that the various Help topics under the selected category are displayed.
	e. In the Topics In "Tables" section, **click the Create A Table link.**
	f. **Scroll down** to view the entire content of the "Create A Table" topic.

2.   Search for a Help topic.

a.   At the top-left corner of the Access Help window, in the Type Words To Search For text box, **type *create a report***

b.   **Click Search.**

c.   Observe that the search results for the keywords "create a report" have been displayed.

d.   In the Results section, **click the Create A Simple Report link** to view its content.

e.   At the top-right corner of the Access Help window, **click the Close button** to close the window.

Lesson 1 Follow-up

In this lesson, you examined the basic database concepts and explored the Access 2007 environment. In addition, you opened an existing Access database and examined the various database objects. Getting acquainted with the Access environment and the database objects will help you use the application with ease.

1. **To store what kind of data would you build a database?**

2. **Which of the user interface components of the Access 2007 application do you think you will use most frequently on the job? Why?**

2 Designing a Database

Lesson Time: 1 hour(s)

Lesson Objectives:

In this lesson, you will design a simple database.

You will:

- Examine the relational database design process.
- Define the purpose of a new database.
- Review existing data.
- Determine the fields to be included in the tables of the database.
- Group fields into tables.
- Normalize the data in a database.
- Designate primary and foreign keys.
- Determine table relationships.

Introduction

In the previous lesson, you examined the various objects within a database. But before creating your first database and using these objects, it is important that you consider the key aspects of good database design. In this lesson, you will examine the steps required to design a database.

Just as you wouldn't attempt to build a house without a blueprint, you shouldn't create a database without a plan. For a simple department intranet database, this design phase may not take very long or require input from very many stakeholders. A large financial or human resources database, on the other hand, would require a lengthy planning phase with input from numerous groups in your organization.

TOPIC A

Describe the Relational Database Design Process

You examined an Microsoft® Office Access™ 2007 database and its components. The structure and design of databases will differ depending on the purpose for which they are created and the data that they contain. However, most well-designed databases are created using a set database design process. In this topic, you will examine the steps in the database design process in order to create databases that will suit your needs.

With any complicated activity, following a well-defined process will help you to stay on track, include all the appropriate inputs, and produce the best possible output. Designing a new database is no different—adhering to the phases of the relational database design process will ensure that your database will do what you want it to and be able to be easily maintained.

The Relational Database Design Process

The relational database design process is a sequential process that can be used to create a design plan for a relational database. It consists of seven stages:

1. Identify the purpose of the database.
2. Review existing data.
3. Make a preliminary list of fields.
4. Organize the fields into tables.
5. Enter sample data, review for possible data maintenance problems, and revise the table design as necessary.
6. Designate primary and foreign keys that can be used to relate your tables together.
7. Determine table relationships.

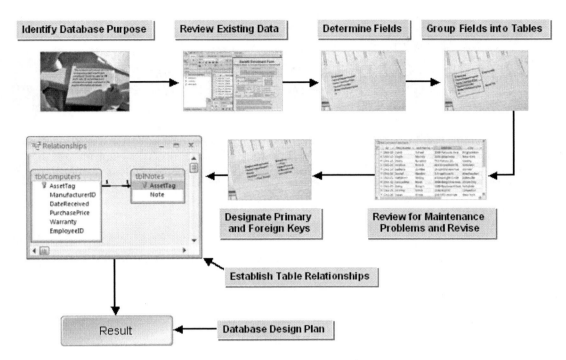

Figure 2-1: The seven stages of database design.

ACTIVITY 2-1

Understanding the Relational Database Design Process

Scenario:

You are designing a database for a client and want to ensure that the database you are creating for them will suit their needs, and is easy to use and maintain. You want to explain the design process to them, so they can be confident of the outcome.

---

1. In a relational database design, what task is performed after review of existing data is completed?

   a) Organizing fields into tables

   b) Designating primary and foreign keys

   c) Identifying the purpose of the database

   d) Making a preliminary list of fields

---

2. Why should you enter sample data into tables after creating them?

   a) To check for potential data maintenance problems

   b) To identify primary and foreign keys

   c) To create a preliminary list of fields

   d) To review existing data

TOPIC B
Define Database Purpose

In the previous topic, you examined the steps in the database design process. You now want to implement the first step in the design process. In this topic, you will determine the purpose you want the database to serve.

As with any activity, if you don't have a clear purpose, you run the risk of going off track, doing too much or too little, or creating something that may not be suitable for your needs. Determining a clear statement of purpose for the database you are designing will keep you on track and help reduce these risks. You can come back to it throughout the design process to help you answer questions that might arise.

The Statement of Purpose

Definition:

A *statement of purpose* is a clear statement that defines the scope of a database and helps to guide its design. It should imply the kinds of data that will be included in the database, but not state specific table or field names. It can describe who the likely types of users of the database will be, but not state specific queries or reports they intend to run. It is sometimes useful to include a statement of what the database will not do.

Example:

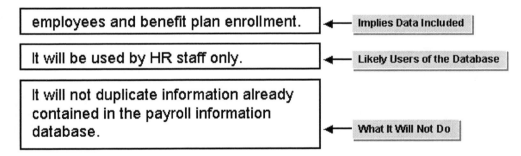

The database will contain information on

employees and benefit plan enrollment.	◄— Implies Data Included
It will be used by HR staff only.	◄— Likely Users of the Database
It will not duplicate information already contained in the payroll information database.	◄— What It Will Not Do

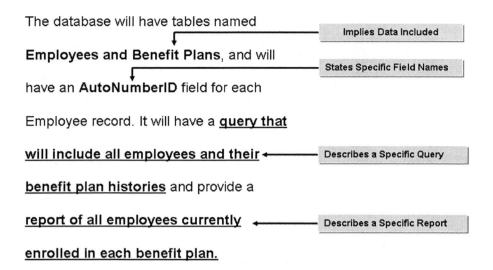

The database will have tables named **Employees and Benefit Plans**, and will have an **AutoNumberID** field for each Employee record. It will have a **query that will include all employees and their benefit plan histories** and provide a **report of all employees currently enrolled in each benefit plan.**

Implies Data Included

States Specific Field Names

Describes a Specific Query

Describes a Specific Report

ACTIVITY 2-2

Understanding a Statement of Purpose

Scenario:

In your new position as head of Information Management for your company, you've decided to create a custom database to track your company's computers and the employees assigned to each of them.

1. **What is wrong with the following statement of purpose?**

   The database will have tables for computers, personnel, manufacturers, product, sales, salaries, and company suggestions.

   a) The statement of purpose should not attempt to list specific tables.

   b) The statement of purpose is too specific.

   c) There is nothing wrong with this statement of purpose.

   d) The statement does not include statements on what the database will not do.

2. **What is wrong with the following statement of purpose?**

   The database will allow the user to generate reports that list the computers used by each employee, as well as queries that sort records by date on which the computer was purchased and the manufacturer of the computer.

   a) It does not discuss the scope of the database.

   b) It does not mention or imply how individual entities in the database will be related.

   c) It discusses specific features (queries and reports) that you would like to see provided.

   d) There is nothing wrong with this statement of purpose.

TOPIC C
Review Existing Data

In the previous topic, you identified the purpose of the database. The next step is to examine the existing data and determine which of it needs to be included in the database to fulfill that purpose. In this topic, you will review existing data.

Although you may think you know exactly what data should be included in the database you are designing, you'll be surprised how often you'll miss something. By considering pre-existing data sources such as paper forms and spreadsheets of data, you can reduce the risk of missing essential data for your database. Also, if any of the data is available in electronic format, you can use it directly in the database.

Existing Data

Existing data is information available for you to review as defined in your statement of purpose, and it falls within the scope of your database. This data can be in paper or electronic format. Existing data in paper format could include internal business forms or documents; third-party or government forms or documents; and printed invoices, bills, or sales slips.

Existing data in electronic format could include spreadsheets such as Microsoft Excel; word processing documents such as Microsoft Word; databases such as Access, SQL Server, or Oracle; and web pages.

 An existing data source may also contain information that is outside the scope of the planned database. Use your statement of purpose to determine this as necessary.

ACTIVITY 2-3
Exploring and Reviewing Existing Data

Scenario:
The statement of purpose for your database is "The database will hold information on the company's inventory of computers and their allocation to employees." In your search for existing data, you find that the Receiving department fills out a ticket for each item that is delivered.

Our Global Company

Receiving Department

Employee Hire Date: _06/30/06_

Item: _Omni desktop computer system_

Notes: _assigned Asset tag # 1266_

For: _Sales department_

---

1. **What are the pieces of data from the sample ticket that you think should be included in your database?**
   a) Company name
   b) Manufacturer name
   c) Asset tag number
   d) Department name

2. **What are the pieces of information found on a receiving ticket that will not be necessary to build a database with this statement of purpose?**

   a) Employee's first and last name

   b) Description of the computer

   c) Employee's hire date

   d) Computer warranty information

TOPIC D
Determine Fields

If you have reviewed existing data, you should have a good start on your field list. To complete the third step in the database design process, you need to determine if any additional fields need to be added to satisfy the statement of purpose. In this topic, you will determine the fields to be included in your database.

You don't want to spend a lot of time creating a database and designing beautiful forms and reports only to find that they don't meet the needs of the consumers of the information. You can prevent this by involving these people in the design and getting as many details as possible about their information needs.

How to Determine Additional Fields

When you appropriately determine additional fields, you will meet your users' needs while staying within the scope of your statement of purpose.

Guidelines

When interviewing the potential users of a database to determine additional fields, be sure to:

- State your database's statement of purpose at the beginning of each conversation to help everyone stay focused.
- Ask questions to gain a better understanding of the fields that will be required:
    - What sort of data do you expect the database to contain?
    - What kinds of reports would you like to be able to generate from the database?
    - What types of summary information do you expect the database to produce?
    - What kind of data analysis needs to be done using the database?

 If you are the only potential user of the database you are designing, then you will need to consider these questions yourself. It is still an essential stage in the process and should not be skipped.

Example:

You are designing a database to track enrollment of employees in benefit plans. You have reviewed existing data and now need to determine additional fields. In interviewing other members of the Human Resources department, you begin by making clear your statement of purpose. You then ask them what kinds of reports they will need to run and what kind of summary information they will need to obtain. They have indicated that they would like to know the number of employees enrolled in a particular plan and how many have joined each plan during each month. As a result of these interviews, you know that you will need to include the Employee Plan and Plan Enroll Date fields.

DISCOVERY ACTIVITY 2-4
Exploring the List of Fields

Scenario:

In your search for existing data, you find that the Receiving department fills out a ticket for each item that is delivered. From the Receiving ticket and other sources, you have been able to arrive at the following list of pre-existing data:

- Employee department
- Purchase date of computer
- Manufacturer
- Note about each computer

The manager of Technical Services would like to get a weekly report of all new computers received and to whom they are assigned, so that she can arrange to set up the hardware. She would also like to know if the system is covered by a warranty. Additionally, the Finance manager would like to obtain a monthly summary of departmental computer hardware purchases.

---

1. **What additional data will you need to include about each employee?**

   a) Name

   b) Salary

   c) Date of birth

   d) Asset tag

---

2. **What additional fields will you need to include in the database to enable the Technical Services manager and the Finance manager to view the weekly and monthly reports, respectively?**

   a) Warranty coverage

   b) Purchase price

   c) Software games included

   d) Configuration of the computer

TOPIC E
Group Fields into Tables

Having defined the purpose of the database and analyzed the existing data, you have identified all the fields you need in the database. You now need to group these fields into tables to create the basic database structure. In this topic, you will organize fields into tables.

Tables are the core objects of any Access database. They are used to store data and are, therefore, the inputs for queries, forms, and reports. To a large extent, table design determines the efficiency of database operations. While you can change the design of tables after they're created, it's much less work to try to get the right table design at the start.

Business Rules

Business rules are a set of policies and procedures that govern the operations of an organization. They clearly define the rules for entering data in a database that are specific to an organization's methods of conducting its operations. The relationships between the various entities in an organizational setup are best described by these business rules.

Business Rules Within an Organization

Assume that your company has an internal policy that computers are assigned to departments rather than to specific employees. This would affect the way you design the tables in a computer inventory tracking database. As you look at existing data, talk to potential users, and group fields into tables, you should be aware of company policies. If you don't already know the pertinent company policies, you should inquire about them.

Field and Table Names

It is usually a good practice to make field and table names brief but descriptive. Access has constraints on field and table names.

Constraint	Description
Name length	The name length cannot exceed 64 characters.
Use of punctuation	Names cannot include a period, an exclamation point, an accent grave, brackets, or double quotation marks.
Use of spaces	Names cannot have a leading space. Access permits you to have spaces within table and field names; however, if there is an internal space, you will have to enclose that table or field name within brackets when you refer to it in expressions and other places. So, you might want to get into the habit of not using spaces in table and field names. One option is to use the underscore character (_) in place of a space in a field name.

How to Group Fields into Tables

Grouping fields into tables will allow you to effectively relate information in your database.

Guidelines

Use these guidelines when grouping fields into tables:

- A table should hold information on only one subject.

- Don't be concerned about having too many tables. It's much more likely that you won't have enough.

- Try to identify tables that correspond to tangible objects, such as people and physical objects. Such entities have properties or attributes that will likely constitute the fields of the table.

- For intangible subjects, try to identify a collection of logically related information with common characteristics.

 If five different database designers followed the recommended design process for the same database, it is entirely possible that they would arrive at five slightly different designs. This is because each individual can have a different thought process and may make different assumptions along the way. That's why the standard design process is so important. It helps ensure that whatever the details of the final design, it will comply with good design principles.

Example: Employees and Benefit Plans Tables

In a database for tracking enrollment of employees in benefit plans, you have one table for employees and another for benefit plans. These are both entities that have related properties. Each employee has a name, department, phone number, employee plan ID, and date of enrollment. Each benefit plan has a plan name, provider, benefits, and description.

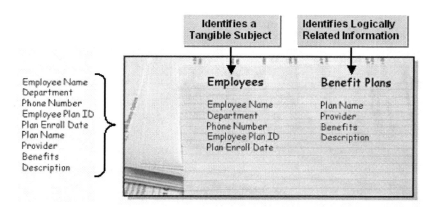

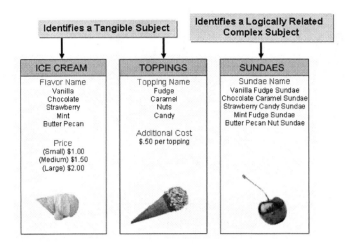

DISCOVERY ACTIVITY 2-5
Understanding How to Group Fields into Tables

Scenario:

You're continuing work on designing your computer inventory database, and you've decided that you need fields such as Employee Name, Asset Tag Number, Computer Manufacturer, Date Received, Computer Note or Comment, Employee Department, Warranty Coverage, and Purchase Price.

Now you need to group them into tables.

---

1. **Based on the information you now have, which two tables would be minimally required for this database?**

   a) Computers and Notes

   b) Computers and Employees

   c) Computers and Departments

   d) Employees and Departments

---

2. **Which fields will be included in an Employees table?**

   a) Name

   b) Computer Manufacturer

   c) Department

   d) Warranty Coverage

---

3. **Which fields will be included in a Computers table?**

   a) Asset Tag Number

   b) Date Received

   c) Employee Name

   d) Purchase Price

TOPIC F
Normalize Data

In the previous topic, you determined the fields to be included in the database, grouped them, and drafted tables. The next step is to enter sample data in these tables to look for any potential problems with maintaining the data. In this topic, you will examine the concept of normalizing data.

Identifying possible data maintenance problems before you enter the actual data in the database and start working with it will save you a lot of trouble and extra work later on. Improperly designed tables can also result in inaccurate data, and you certainly don't want to make decisions based on data that you can't trust.

Normalization

Definition:

Normalization is the process of organizing data in a database to produce optimized table structures. It usually involves refining a database by reducing complex data in a table into simple and stable table structures. Normalization ensures data integrity in tables by eliminating two issues: data redundancy and inconsistent dependency between them.

Example:

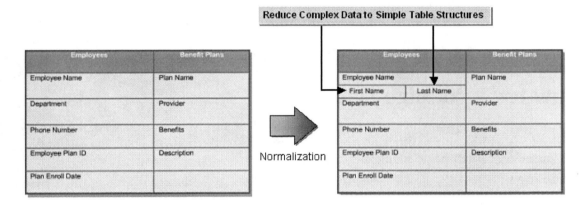

Figure 2-2: Normalization helps break down complex data structures into simpler ones.

Denormalization
Definition:

Denormalization is a database performance optimization process that adds redundant data to tables to speed up database access. During denormalization, data is combined into one table, which is otherwise presented in two different tables as indicated by the normalization process. A database designer may denormalize data to make queries run faster against very large tables, keep similar data together, and keep the overall table structure simple.

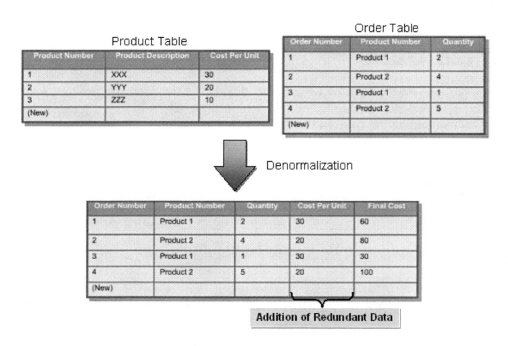

Figure 2-3: Denormalization increases database efficiency by adding redundant data to tables.

Example:

A common example of denormalization is allowing an occasional field to be blank for some records. For instance, a database may contain a Middle Initial field, but not all employees have or use a middle initial. Strict normalization rules would state that the field should not be null— but it is common practice to keep this field in the same table with the first and last names.

How to Normalize Data

Data normalization ensures that when you implement the tables you have planned, the resulting database will be able to efficiently provide the queries and reports desired, and ongoing data maintenance will be as simple as possible.

Guidelines

The following are common data normalization guidelines:

● Each field should contain the smallest meaningful value.

● There should be no repeated groups of fields.

● Data values should not be repeated unnecessarily.

● When reasonable, all fields in a record should contain a value.

Non-Example:

In the following example, the fields are not normalized. The Name field can be broken down further into meaningful parts. There are two Email Address fields, and the second will not always have a value.

● Full Name

● Work Phone Number

● Work Email Address 1

● Work Email Address 2

- Social Security Number
- Begin Date

Example:

In the following example, each field has the smallest meaningful value, there are no repeated groups of fields or repeated data values, and every record in the table will have a value in each of these fields.

- Employee First Name
- Employee Last Name
- Work Phone Number
- Work Email Address
- Social Security Number
- Begin Date

DISCOVERY ACTIVITY 2-6

Exploring Data Maintenance Problems

Scenario:

You have two draft tables for the computer inventory database. One is called Employees and the other that you have decided upon is called Computers. Each table has six fields. You have been asked to review the table design and prepare a report on any potential problems that you foresee in the design.

1.

Table: Employees		
EmployeeName	**DepartmentName**	**DeptCode**
Jason Smith	Administration	A1
Lyn McMillan	Administration	A1
Amy Wang	Fulfillment	F1
Andrea Brown	Sales	S1
Susan Kilinski	Fulfillment	F1

What should be done with the EmployeeName field to normalize data?

   a) It should be made to list the last name first, with a comma, and then the first name.

   b) It should be broken up into two separate fields: one for the first name and one for the last name.

   c) It should be made to include the last name data only.

   d) Nothing needs to be done; it is fully normalized as it is.

2. **True or False? Since the DepartmentName field holds repeated values, a Departments table should hold these values.**

   ___ True

   ___ False

3.

Table: Computers					
AssetTag	ManufacturerID	DateReceived	PurchasePrice	Warranty	Notes
1020	3	1/5/2005	$3,200	☑	Notes
1047	4	8/20/2005	$1,499	☐	
1055	3	9/7/2005	$2,700	☐	Desktop
1066	3	11/7/2005	$3,200	☑	
1073	2	12/1/2005	$1,200	☐	Laptop

True or False? Since not all records have an entry in the Notes field, strict adherence to normalization guidelines would require that the Notes field be moved to a separate table.

___ True

___ False

4. **What can be done to normalize the data in the ManufacturerID field?**

 a) The entries should all be alphabetic.

 b) The entries should all be alphanumeric.

 c) Since it has repeated entries, there should be a Manufacturers table to hold that data.

 d) Nothing; it is completely normalized already.

5. **What needs to be done to normalize the Warranty field's data?**

 a) It should be a text field.

 b) Because some check boxes are not checked, the data is in a separate table.

 c) Nothing; it is fully normalized already.

 d) More fields pertaining to warranty need to be included in the same table.

OPTIONAL DISCOVERY ACTIVITY 2-7
Understanding Normalization of Data

Scenario:
Your coworker is working on some tables that contain employee and project-related data. He has asked you to help him normalize these tables in his databases.

1.

EmployeeID	FirstName	LastName	DeptCode	Address
0026	Jason	Smith	300	12, Sunshine Dr. New York, NY - 11123
0027	Lyn	McMillan	300	34, Highland Avenue, Stanford, CT - 62024
0032	Amy	Wang	300	555, Dew Avenue, New York, NY - 11135

Which field needs to be broken down further to the smallest meaningful unit?

   a) LastName
   b) FirstName
   c) DeptCode
   d) Address

2. **Based on the data shown, which additional fields would you need to add to normalize the Address field?**

   a) City
   b) State
   c) Zip Code
   d) Country

3.

Employee-Project Time Allocation					
LastName	FirstName	Project 1	Time 1	Project 2	Time 2
Smith	Jason	AA755	90	AA60	70
McMillan	Lyn	AA750	40	AA45	45
Wang	Amy	AA760	60	AA700	75
Brown	Andrea	AA740	20	AA300	70

What are the data normalization problems in this table?

a) The LastName field appears before the FirstName field.

b) There is a repeated group of Project fields.

c) There is a repeated group of Time fields.

d) The sets of Project and Time fields are not adjacent.

4.

Table: Project Details			
Project Number	Project Name	Project Manager	Phone
AA755	Benefits Handbook	Jason	7232
AA750	Recognition Program	Lyn	7443
AA760	Appraisal Process	Amy	7233
AA740	Warehouse Rack System	Andrea	7311

What are the data maintenance problems that this design can cause?

a) The project names are too long.

b) You would need to edit phone numbers in more than one record.

c) Storing only the first name of a person might lead to ambiguity in cases where there are two people with the same first name.

d) The project naming convention is incorrect.

5. **True or False? You could normalize the data by moving the Project Manager and Phone fields into a second, but related, table.**

___ True

___ False

TOPIC G
Designate Primary and Foreign Keys

You've modified the design of the tables so that you're confident data can be maintained accurately. The next step in database design is to identify fields that can be used to relate these tables. In this topic, you will identify such fields and designate them as primary and foreign keys.

As in any other relational database management system, Access databases have great querying power, owing to the relationship set between the tables in the database. Properly assigning primary and foreign keys is essential to creating useful relationships between your tables.

Primary Keys

Definition:

A *primary key* is a field that contains unique values, which are used to identify each record. This key is used to establish appropriate relationships between tables. Primary key fields can be of any data type, except for Memo, OLE Object, or Attachment, and can never be left blank, which means there will never be any missing or unknown values. Also, they have values that rarely change, and do not allow duplicates.

 AutoNumber is a common datatype choice for primary key fields because it guarantees uniqueness.

Example: EmployeeID as a Primary Key

Figure 2-4: An EmployeeID field is a good candidate for being a primary key for an Employees table.

 Other common examples of primary key fields include Student ID Number, Order Number, Item Code, Part Number, Serial Number, ISBN Number, and Date Plus Time.

Non-Example:

A LastName field is not a good primary key field because it can have duplicate values. An email field is not a good primary key field either, because it could allow for blank values and changes often.

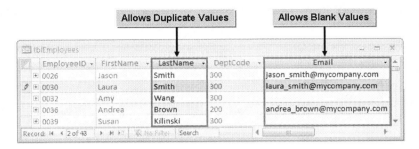

Figure 2-5: Not all fields would be good primary keys.

Composite Keys

Definition:

A *composite key* is a primary key that is formed as a combination of two or more fields that uniquely identify a record. A composite key is known by several other names such as a compound or concatenated key. Similar to a single field primary key, a composite key will not allow duplicate values.

Example:

Assume that you have a table that holds details of various projects undertaken in the company.

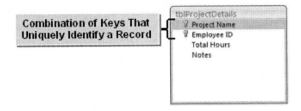

Figure 2-6: A composite key is a combination of two or more fields.

None of the fields in the tblProjectDetails table have the capability to uniquely identify a record. In such situations, you could choose the ProjectName and EmployeeID fields as a composite key to help you uniquely identify each record.

Foreign Keys

Definition:

A *foreign key* is a field or combination of fields in a table and relates to a primary key field of another table. Its data type must match that of the related primary key field. Duplicate values can appear in the foreign key field. The combination of primary and foreign key fields is what gives Access its strength to query information.

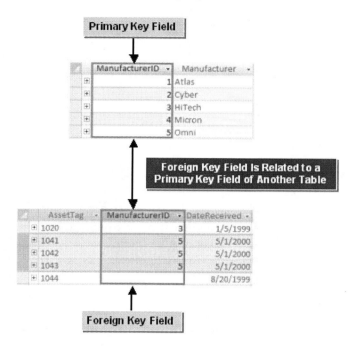

Figure 2-7: A foreign key field is related to the primary key field of another table.

Example:

Consider two tables: Employees and Departments. The common attribute that relates these two tables is DeptCode. Here, the DeptCode field is the primary key of the Department table as it is unique and each of the many values of this field occur just once. The values of the DeptCode field of the Employees table tend to repeat for employees working in the same department and therefore will be designated as the foreign key.

Need for Primary and Foreign Keys

One of the prime reasons for defining a primary key is related to the fact that it acts as an index for all records. Further, it helps to implement a relationship between two tables in a relational database. The foreign key, on the other hand, helps you establish a relationship with a primary key table to enable you to retrieve matching records.

Using Primary and Foreign Keys

In a database, the information relating to one entity may be spread across two or more tables. For example, in a bank, you can store a customer's details in two different tables: Personal and Transactions. In the Personal table, you will be storing personal information about a customer. In the Transactions table, you will be storing information pertaining to the banking transactions of the customer.

A CustomerID field in the Personal table will occur just once, and it will be designated as the primary key. The CustomerID will have multiple occurrences in the Transaction table depending on the number of transactions done by the customer over a period of time.

You may want to retrieve details about the customers. As part of the process, you will retrieve all personal information, such as name and address from the Personal table, and the list of transactions from the Transactions table for a particular customer. This is easily achieved by comparing the CustomerID fields of both the tables and displaying those relevant records.

ACTIVITY 2-8
Identifying Primary and Foreign Key Fields

Scenario:
Your database design contains the Employees, Departments, Computers, Manufacturers, and Notes tables. The Employees table contains the FirstName, LastName, and DeptCode fields. The Departments table contains the DeptCode and Department fields. The Manufacturers table contains the ManufacturerID, and Manufacturer fields. The Notes table contains the AssetTag and Notes fields. The Computers table contains the AssetTag, DateReceived, PurchasePrice, and Warranty fields. Now, you need to designate which fields will be primary keys and, where necessary, foreign keys. In doing so, you are preparing your tables to be properly related together.

1. **Which field in the Employees table would be the most suitable for a primary key?**
   a) LastName
   b) FirstName
   c) DeptCode
   d) A new field, EmployeeID

2. **In which table should the EmployeeID field appear as a foreign key field?**
   a) Departments
   b) Computers
   c) Manufacturers
   d) Notes

3. **Which field can be designated as the primary key for the Departments table?**
   a) EmployeeID
   b) DeptCode
   c) Department
   d) Department Manager

4. **Which table should have DeptCode as a foreign key field?**
   a) Employees
   b) Computers
   c) Manufacturers
   d) Notes

5. **If you were to add a ManufacturerID field to serve as the primary field for the Manufacturers table, what other table should have a ManufacturerID field as a foreign key?**

    a) Employees

    b) Departments

    c) Computers

    d) Notes

TOPIC H
Determine Table Relationships

In the previous topic, you designated the primary and foreign keys for your table. The next step in implementing your database design will be to establish appropriate relationships between tables. In this topic, you will establish relationships between various tables in your database.

You can't harness the full power of a relational database management system such as Access without establishing table relationships. Establishing table relationships helps you ensure the accuracy of data, and enables the breadth of queries and reports that you will likely want to use to retrieve, display, and print your data.

Table Relationships

Table relationships are a representation of the association between data contained within tables. Defining table relationships will help you pull records from related tables based on matching fields. The matching fields are better known as primary and foreign keys.

Need for Table Relationships

After creating tables in your database, you need to retrieve the information when needed. This is done by placing common fields in tables that are related and by defining relationships among your tables. Defining table relationships helps you create queries, forms, and reports that display information from several tables all at once. They further act as a foundation for ensuring the integrity of the data stored in your database.

The One-to-One Relationship

Definition:

A *one-to-one relationship* is a relationship between two tables where both the primary key and the foreign key are unique. For each record in the first table, there will be one and only one record in the second table. In this relationship, the entity from which a relationship originates is the parent entity and the other is the child entity.

Example:

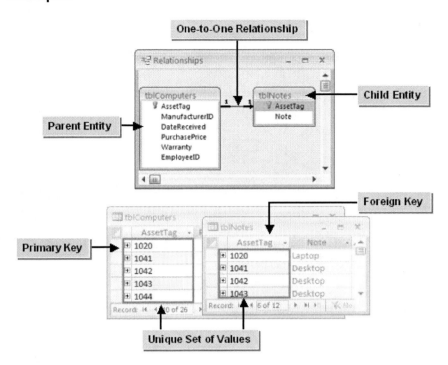

Figure 2-8: A one-to-one relationship between two tables, using the AssetTag field as the key.

The One-to-Many Relationship

Definition:

A *one-to-many relationship* is a relationship between two tables where the primary key is unique, but the foreign key allows duplicate values. For each record in the primary key table, there can be multiple records in the foreign key table.

Example:

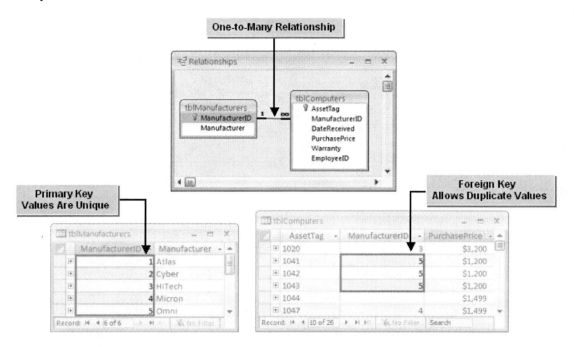

Figure 2-9: A one-to-many relationship between a tblManufacturers table and a tblComputers table, using the ManufacturerID field as the key.

ACTIVITY 2-9

Examining Table Relationships

Scenario:

Your database design now contains the Employees, Departments, Computers, Manufacturers, and Notes tables. The primary and foreign keys have been designated. You need to enhance the design of the database to enable users to retrieve relevant data from related tables.

---

1. The values for the DeptCode field have a single occurrence in the Departments table and multiple occurrences in the Employees table. What kind of relationship exists between the two tables?

   a) One-to-one

   b) One-to-many

   c) Many-to-one

   d) Many-to-many

---

2. The values for the AssetTag field in the Computers table have a corresponding single value in the Notes table. What kind of relationship exists between the two tables?

   a) One-to-one

   b) One-to-many

   c) Many-to-one

   d) Many-to-many

Lesson 2 Follow-up

In this lesson, you examined the steps required to plan a simple Microsoft® Office Access™ 2007 database. You followed a process that ensures your resulting database will take into account existing data, fulfill the needs of users, and be both robust and easy to maintain. You can feel confident that the design you now have can be implemented as an Access database appropriate to your goals.

1. **Why is it important to create a plan before building your database?**

2. **What fields would you include in the first database you need to build on your job? How would you group them into tables?**

3 | **Building a Database**

Lesson Time: 1 hour(s), 15 minutes

Lesson Objectives:

In this lesson, you will build a new database with related tables.

You will:

● Create a new database.

● Create a new table.

● Manage tables.

● Create relationships between tables.

● Save a database as a previous version.

Introduction

In the previous lesson, you designed a database. You may need to build the database using Access. In this lesson, you will build a new database.

A database design is similar to a software blueprint. Just as programmers need to code the program, you need to build the structure of your database. Building a database from scratch will give you more flexibility. But to create a solid structure, you should use your design as a strict guide to ensure that you don't deviate from the statement of purpose.

TOPIC A
Create a New Database

You created a database design using the principles of relational database design. The next step is to actually create a database using a database application, such as Access. In this topic, you will create a new database.

After you have designed your database, you may find that an existing Access database template offers a structure that is a good fit for your data. In such cases, you may want to create a database using the template to save time. However, if your data and workflow do not map to any of the existing database templates, you may have to create a database from scratch. Access has several database templates that you can choose from. It also has an option for building a new database.

Access Database Templates

Access provides several predefined database templates that can be used to create a new database. Each template provides a design that will serve a specific purpose. These templates consist of the underlying tables, as well as the queries, forms, and reports that are based on these tables. A basic set of templates is installed on your computer when you install Access.

How to Create a New Database

Procedure Reference: Create a Blank Database

To create a blank database:

1. In the Getting Started With Microsoft Office Access window, in the middle pane, in the New Blank Database section, click Blank Database.
2. In the right pane in the Blank Database section, in the File Name text box, type the desired database name.
3. If necessary, specify the location where you want to store the new database.
   a. Click the Browse For A Location To Put Your Database button.
   b. In the File New Database dialog box, navigate to the desired folder.
   c. Click OK.
4. Click Create to create a blank database.

Procedure Reference: Create a Template-Based Database

To create a database from a template:

1. In the Getting Started With Microsoft Office Access window, in the left pane, in the From Microsoft Office Online section, select the desired category.
2. In the middle pane, select the desired template.
3. In the right pane, in the File Name text box, type the desired database name.
4. If necessary, specify the location where you want to store the new database.
5. Click Download to open the template-based database.

ACTIVITY 3-1

Creating a New Database

Before You Begin:

1. In the Access Options dialog box, select the Datasheet category.

2. In the Default Colors section, click the Font Color drop-down button and select Automatic.

3. Click the Background Color drop-down button and select Automatic.

4. In the Access Options dialog box, click OK.

Scenario:

As the Accounts Manager of your company, you want to store the purchase information of computers that are bought every year. Also, you want to store the contact details of agents who supply the hardware equipment to your company.

What You Do	How You Do It
1. Create a blank database.	a. In the middle pane, in the New Blank Database section, **click Blank Database.**
	b. In the right pane, in the Blank Database section, in the File Name text box, **triple-click and type *MyComputerInventory.accdb***
	c. Below the File Name text box, observe that the location in which the new file is going to be saved is displayed.
	d. **Click the Browse For A Location To Put Your Database button.**
	e. In the File New Database dialog box, **navigate to the C:\084887Data\Building a Database folder and click OK.**
	f. **Click Create.**
	g. Observe that a blank database has been created and the name of the new database is displayed on the title bar. The title bar also indicates that the database is in Access 2007 file format. As a blank database, there are no queries, forms, or reports created yet.
	h. **Close the blank database.**

2. Create a template-based database.

a. In the left pane, observe that the various categories of database templates are listed.

b. In the From Microsoft Office Online section, **select Business.**

c. In the middle pane, in the Business section, **select Contacts.**

d. In the right pane, in the Contacts section, in the File Name text box, **triple-click and type *MyClientContacts.accdb***

e. **Click the Browse For A Location To Put Your Database button.**

f. In the File New Database dialog box, **navigate to the C:\084887Data\Building a Database folder and click OK.**

g. **Click Download** to open the template-based database.

h. If necessary, in the Microsoft Office Genuine Advantage message box, **click Continue.**

i. **Close the Access Help window.**

j. Observe that a new database based on the Contacts template is created.

k. **Expand the Navigation Pane.**

l. **Click the Navigation Pane drop-down arrow and select Object Type** to display all the objects in the database.

m. Observe that the Contacts template has provided you with one table, one query, two forms, and two reports, thereby saving you the time and effort that would have been otherwise needed to create those objects from scratch.

n. **Close the database.**

TOPIC B
Create a Table

In the previous topic, you performed a series of steps to design tables in your database. However, before you go ahead and store data in them, you need to create these tables in your Access database. In this topic, you will create a table to store data.

After designing your tables, you can now to create them. Assume that you want to create a table to hold your product details. You can use either an existing template or an existing data source, such as a spreadsheet, if they fit your design requirements. On the other hand, you can create one from scratch. In either case, you will have to ensure that you don't face data maintenance problems at a later stage.

Table Views

Based on the operations that you might want to perform on a table, Access offers you different kinds of table views. The most commonly used views are Datasheet and Design.

In the Design view, you will be able to view all the fields with their data types and descriptions. The records within the table are not displayed in this view. When a field is selected in this view, the properties for that field are displayed at the bottom of the window. You can manipulate the properties of a field by setting the field properties in the Field Properties pane during design time.

The Datasheet view is the default view, and it displays the records in a table similar to a spreadsheet. Each row constitutes a single record. The column headers are the field names derived from the table's definition.

The Field Insertion Feature

In Access 2007, you can use the *Field Insertion* feature to easily insert a new field by typing the field name in the first row of a new column in Datasheet view. This feature will enable you to quickly create a table structure, even if you do not know the intricacies of a database.

Data Types

Each field in a table can be designed to hold a particular kind of data value called a *data type*.

Commonly Used Data Type	Description
Text	A Text field can contain values that are text, numbers, or a combination of both. The maximum length of each value is 255 characters.
Memo	A Memo field is an advancement to the Text field. You can store up to 2 GB of data for a Memo field. Memo fields support rich-text formatting such as bold, italics, and bulleted lists.
Number	A Number field can hold number values up to 16 bytes of data.

Commonly Used Data Type	Description
Date/Time	A Date/Time field is used to store and manipulate date and time information.
Currency	A Currency field can store values of monetary type.
AutoNumber	An AutoNumber is a field containing unique values and is created automatically by Access when you create a new record. AutoNumber fields are typically used as primary keys.
Yes/No	The Yes/No field contains Boolean (true or false) data. Access uses -1 for all Yes values and 0 for all No values.
Hyperlink	The Hyperlink field helps you store web addresses. The maximum limit of storage is 1 GB of data. You can store links to websites as well as sites or files on an intranet or Local Area Network.
Attachment	An Attachment field is used to attach images, spreadsheet files, documents, charts, and other types of supported files to the records in your database. Access allows you to attach files to records only if the database is in 2007 format. You can also detach an attachment and navigate through the different attachments within a record.

[Handwritten margin notes: "provides a higher level of accuracy. will only do this to 4 decimal places." "unique number." "(Not a link. – it is a copy of the attached data.) Scan to PDF not tiff"]

File Types Supported by the Attachment Data Type

Access supports all file formats created using Microsoft Office 2007. Access also supports file formats such as .bmp, .gif, and .jpeg. However, certain file formats such as .com, .exe, .ins, .scr, and .asp are not allowed in Access.

Multivalued Fields

A *multivalued field* enables you to store multiple values in a field. You can create a multivalued field using the Lookup Wizard. In the wizard, you can either type the desired value or take the desired value from a table or a query. With the Allow Multiple Values check box in the wizard, you can store multiple values for the lookup.

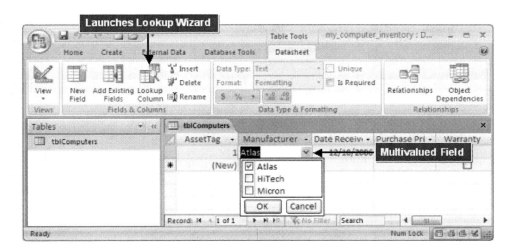

Figure 3-1: Multivalued fields allow you to store more than one value.

File Types

Access allows you to save a table separately for future use in two specified file formats: Portable Document Format (PDF) and XML Paper Specification (XPS).

In order to use the PDF or XPS feature available with Microsoft Office 2007, you will have to download and install the Microsoft Save As PDF Or XPS add-in. This add-in is available on the Microsoft website.

File Format	Description
Portable Document Format (PDF)	A PDF is a fixed layout file format formed as an electronic image of a print document. It preserves document formatting and enables file sharing. The PDF format ensures that, when the file is viewed online or printed, it retains the same format as the original document and that data in the file cannot be easily tampered with.
XML Paper Specification (XPS)	Similar to the Portable Document Format, XPS is also a file format formed as an electronic image of the original document. It preserves document format and enables file sharing. To view a file in XPS format, you need an XPS viewer.

How to Create a Table

Procedure Reference: Create a Blank Table

To create a blank table:

1. On the Create tab, in the Tables group, click Table.
2. Save the table.
   a. Display the Save As dialog box.
      - On the Quick Access toolbar, click the Save button.
      - Or, click the Office button and choose Save.
   b. In the Save As dialog box, in the Table Name text box, type the desired name.
   c. Click OK.

Procedure Reference: Create a Table Using a Template

To create a table using a template:

1. On the Create tab, in the Tables group, click Table Templates.
2. Select the desired template to open a new table based on the selected template.
3. Save the table.

Procedure Reference: Create a Table Based on the Structure of an Existing Table in a Different Database

To create a table based on the structure of an existing table in a different database:

1. In the Navigation Pane, right-click the desired table and choose Export→Access Database.
2. In the Export - Access Database dialog box, click Browse to choose the database to which you want to export the structure of the selected table.
3. In the File Save dialog box, navigate to the folder in which the database (to which you want to export the selected table's structure) is located and select the desired database.
4. Click Save.
5. In the Export - Access Database dialog box, click OK.
6. In the Export dialog box, in the Export Tables section, select the Definition Only option and click OK to export the selected table's structure.
7. In the Export - Access Database dialog box, click Close.
8. If desired, open the database to which you exported the table structure and verify the table was created.

Procedure Reference: Create a Table Based on the Structure of an Existing Table in the Same Database

To create a table based on the structure of an existing table in the same database:

1. In the Navigation Pane, right-click the desired table and choose Copy.
2. In the Navigation Pane, right-click and choose Paste.
3. In the Paste Table As dialog box, type the name for the new table, select Structure Only, and click OK.

Procedure Reference: Insert a Field and a Record in a Table

To insert a field and a record in a table:

1. Open the desired table.

2. Insert a field in the table.

- In the table, double-click Add New Field and type the desired field name.
- Insert a field using the Field Templates task pane.

    a. On the Ribbon, select the Table Tools Datasheet contextual tab.

    b. In the Fields & Columns group, click New Field.

    c. In the Field Templates task pane, from the desired section, double-click the desired field to add it to the table.

- Or, insert a field in the table in Design view.

    a. Switch to Design view.

    - On the Home tab, in the Views group, click the View button.
    - Or, on the Home tab, in the Views group, click the View drop-down arrow and select Design View.

    b. In the design grid, in the Field Name column, in the desired cell, type the desired field name.

3. If necessary, switch to Design view.

4. In the design grid, click in the Data Type column next to the newly inserted field, and from the Data Type drop-down list, select the desired option.

5. If necessary, set the field as a primary key.

    a. Move the mouse pointer to before the newly inserted field, and when the mouse pointer turns into an arrow, click to select the field.

    b. On the Design contextual tab, in the Tools group, click Primary Key to set the primary key for the selected field.

 In Design view, select the keys you want to designate as the composite key, and in the Tools group, on the Design contextual tab, click Primary Key to designate the composite key for the selected fields.

6. Insert a record.

    a. Switch to Datasheet view.

    - On the Home tab, in the Views group, click the View button.
    - Or, on the Home tab, in the Views group, click the View drop-down arrow and select Datasheet View.

    b. In the table, specify the desired values in all the fields.

Procedure Reference: Create a Multivalued Field

To create a multivalued field:

1. Display the desired table in Design view.

2. In the design grid, click in the Data Type column next to the desired field, and from the Data Type drop-down list, select Lookup Wizard.

3. In the Lookup Wizard dialog box, select the I Will Type In The Values That I Want option to specify the desired values and click Next.

4. In the list box, specify the necessary values and click Next.

5. Check the Allow Multiple Values check box to display multiple values.

6.   Click Finish.

Procedure Reference: Work with an Attachment Field in a Table

To work with an Attachment field in a table:

1.   Open the desired table.

2.   Add an Attachment field.

*   Add an Attachment field in Datasheet view.

    a.   If necessary, switch to Datasheet view.

    b.   On the Table Tools Datasheet contextual tab, in the Fields & Columns group, click New Field to display the Field Templates task pane.

    c.   In the Field Templates task pane, in the Tasks section, double-click Attachments to add an Attachment field to the table.

*   Add an Attachment field to a table in Design View.

    a.   If necessary, switch to Design view.

    b.   In the design grid, type the desired field name in the Field Name column.

    c.   Click in the Data Type column next to the newly added field name, and from the Data Type drop-down list, select Attachment.

    d.   If necessary, in the Field Properties pane, on the General tab, in the Caption text box, type the desired caption.

    e.   Save the changes made to the table design.

3.   Attach files to an Attachment field in a record.

    a.   Display the Attachments dialog box.

    *   In the table, in the desired record, double-click the Attachment icon.

    *   Or, in the table, in the desired record, right-click the Attachment icon and choose Manage Attachments.

    b.   In the Attachments dialog box, click Add.

    c.   In the Choose File dialog box, navigate to the folder that contains the files that are to be attached, select the desired files, and click Open.

    d.   In the Attachments dialog box, click OK to attach the files to the record.

 You can select and attach multiple files to a record.

4.   If desired, export an attachment from a record.

    a.   Display the Attachments dialog box, and in the Attachments (Double-click To Open) list box, select the desired document and click Save As.

    b.   In the Save Attachment dialog box, navigate to the desired folder, name the file as desired, and click Save.

    c.   In the Attachments dialog box, click OK to close the dialog box.

5. If necessary, remove an attachment from a record.

    a. Display the Attachments dialog box, and in the Attachments (Double-click To Open) list box, select the desired document and click Remove.

    b. In the Attachments dialog box, click OK to close the dialog box.

Procedure Reference: Display or Hide the Auto Calendar Icon

To display the Auto Calendar icon:

1. Open the table in Design view and select the desired field with a data type of Date/Time.

2. In the Field Properties pane, on the General tab, from the Show Date Picker drop-down list, select For Dates to display the Auto Calendar icon, or Never to hide the icon.

Procedure Reference: Save a Table as an XPS File

To save a table as an XPS file:

1. In the Navigation Pane, select the desired table.

2. Click the Office button and choose Save As→PDF Or XPS.

3. In the Publish As PDF Or XPS dialog box, navigate to the folder in which you want to save the file, and if necessary, in the File Name text box, type the desired name.

4. From the Save As Type drop-down list, select XPS Document.

5. In the Optimize For section, select the desired option and click Publish to save the table as an XPS document.

ACTIVITY 3-2

Creating a Table

Data Files:

Config_2GHz.doc, Config_3GHz.doc

Before You Begin:

From the C:\084887Data\Building a Database folder, open the MyComputerInventory.accdb file.

Scenario:

You have created a blank database to record your company's inventory information. Now, you want to create a table to store the purchase information of computers in that database. You would also like to document the manufacturers of different parts of each computer purchased. Also, you would like to include the configuration details about each purchased item and publish that information on your company's website and in the annual report.

What You Do	How You Do It
1. Create a blank table.	a. On the Ribbon, **select the Create tab.**
	b. On the Create tab, in the Tables group, **click Table** to create a new table.
2. Save the table.	a. On the Quick Access toolbar, **click the Save button.**
	b. In the Save As dialog box, in the Table Name text box, **type *tblComputers*
	c. **Click OK.**
3. Insert a field into the table.	a. In the tblComputers table, **double-click the ID field heading, type *AssetTag* and press Enter.**
	b. Observe that the AssetTag field has been inserted into the table.

4.	**Add a field to the table using the Field Templates task pane.**	a.	On the Datasheet contextual tab, in the Fields & Columns group, **click New Field.**
		b.	In the Field Templates task pane, in the Assets section, **double-click Manufacturer.**
		c.	In the Field Templates task pane, **click the Close button** to close the Field Templates task pane.
		d.	In the tblComputers table, **double-click the Manufacturer field heading, type *Parts Manufacturers* and press Enter** to rename the Manufacturer field according to your design needs.
5.	**Add fields to the table in Design view.**	a.	On the Home tab, in the Views group, **click the View drop-down arrow and select Design View.**
		b.	In the tblComputers design grid, in the Field Name column, in the third cell, **type *Date Received***
		c.	In the Field Name column, in the fourth cell, **type *Purchase Price***
		d.	In the Field Name column, in the fifth cell, **type *Warranty***
6.	**Set the data types.**	a.	In the Data Type column, **verify that the data type next to AssetTag is AutoNumber, and the data type next to Parts Manufacturers is Text.**
		b.	**Click in the Data Type column next to Date Received,** and from the Data Type drop-down list, **select Date/Time.**
		c.	**Click in the Data Type column next to Purchase Price,** and from the Data Type drop-down list, **select Currency.**
		d.	**Click in the Data Type column next to Warranty,** and from the Data Type drop-down list, **select Yes/No.**

7.   Create a multivalued field.

    a.   **Click in the Data Type column next to Parts Manufacturers,** and from the Data Type drop-down list, **select Lookup Wizard.**

    b.   In the Lookup Wizard dialog box, **select the I Will Type In The Values That I Want option and click Next.**

    c.   In Col1, in the first cell, **type** *Atlas*

    d.   In the second and third cells in the same column, **type** *HiTech* **and** *Micron* **and then click Next.**

    e.   **Check the Allow Multiple Values check box and click Finish.**

    f.   In the Microsoft Office Access warning box, **click Yes.**

8.   Create an Attachment field to store system configuration details.

    a.   In the Field Name column, in the sixth cell, **type** *Configuration Details*

    b.   **Click in the Data Type column,** and from the Data Type drop-down list, **select Attachment.**

    c.   In the Field Properties pane, on the General tab, in the Caption text box, **type** *Configuration*

    d.   **Save the changes to the table design.**

    e.   In the Views group, **click the View drop-down arrow and select Datasheet view** to switch to the Datasheet view.

9. **Insert a record into the table, then attach documents to the Configuration Details field.**

a. In the Parts Manufacturers column, **click in the first cell,** and in the drop-down list, **check the Atlas check box.**

b. **Click OK.**

c. In the AssetTag column, observe that number "1" is automatically entered because the data type of that field is AutoNumber.

d. **Press Enter**, and next to the Date Received column, **click the Auto Calendar icon.** ▦

e. **Navigate to a date six months prior to the current date, select it, and then press Enter.**

f. In the Purchase Price column, **type *8200* and press Enter.**

g. **Check the Warranty check box and press Enter.**

h. **Double-click the Attachment icon** [0̸] to display the Attachments dialog box.

i. In the Attachments dialog box, **click Add.**

j. If necessary, in the Choose File dialog box, **navigate to the C:\084887Data\ Building a Database folder.**

k. **Select Config-2GHz.docx, hold down Shift, and select Config-3GHz.docx to** select these two Word documents.

l. **Click Open.**

m. In the Attachments dialog box, **verify that the selected documents are displayed in the Attachments (Double-click To Open) list box and click OK** to attach them to the record.

n. Observe that the Attachment icon now displays the number 2, indicating that the field contains two documents.

10. **Export an attachment having configuration details about 2 GHz and open the attachment having configuration details about the 3 GHz item.**

a. **Double-click the Attachment icon.**

b. In the Attachments dialog box, in the Attachments (Double-click To Open) list box, **select Config-2GHz.docx and click Save As** to display the Save Attachment dialog box.

c. **Navigate to the C:\084887Data\Building a Database folder, triple-click and type *My Config-2GHz.docx* in the File Name text box, and then click Save.**

d. In the Attachments (Double-click To Open) list box, **double-click Config-3GHz.docx** to open the file.

e. Observe that the attachment has opened in Microsoft Office Word.

f. **Close the Word application.**

g. In the Attachments dialog box, **click OK** to close it.

11. **Save the table as an XPS document.**

a. **Click the Office button and choose Save As→PDF Or XPS.**

b. In the Publish As PDF Or XPS dialog box, **navigate to the C:\084887Data\Building a Database folder.**

c. In the File Name text box, **type *My tblComputers*, and from the Save As Type drop-down list, select XPS Document (*.xps).**

d. In the Optimize For section, **select the Standard (Publishing Online And Printing) option.**

e. **Click Publish** to save the table as an XPS document.

f. **Close the table.**

ACTIVITY 3-3

Creating a Table Using a Template

Before You Begin:
The MyComputerInventory.accdb file is open.

Scenario:
You want to store information about the status of the various projects that are being handled by your company. As you have only a day to create the table and populate it with data, you want to use the quickest method possible in order to finish the task. Also, you want to store the data in such a way that you can access records based on a particular set of fields.

What You Do	How You Do It
1. Open and then save a template-based table.	a. On the Create tab, in the Tables group, **click Table Templates and select Tasks.**
	b. Notice that a new table with predefined fields is displayed.
	c. On the Quick Access toolbar, **click the Save button.**
	d. In the Save As dialog box, **type tblProjects and click OK.**

2. **Change the primary key to a composite key.**

a. On the Home tab, in the Views group, **click the View button** to switch to Design view.

b. In the tblProjects design grid, observe that the key icon is present just before the ID field, indicating that this field is the primary key.

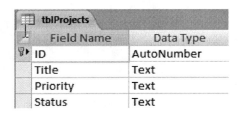

c. **Move the mouse pointer to before the ID field,** and when it turns into an arrow, **click** to select the ID row.

d. **Hold down Shift, and move the mouse pointer to before the Title field,** and when the mouse pointer turns into an arrow, **click** to select the Title row.

e. On the Design contextual tab, in the Tools group, **click Primary Key.**

f. Observe that the key icon also appears before the Title field, indicating that the primary key has been changed to a composite key.

g. **Save the table.**

h. **Close the database.**

ACTIVITY 3-4

Creating a Table Based on the Structure of an Existing Table

Data Files:

Source.accdb, MyComputerInventory.accdb

Before You Begin:

From the C:\084887Data\Building a Database folder, open the Source.accdb file.

Scenario:

You want to store information about the employees who have joined your company in the past six months in a separate table. For easy identification and retrieval of data, you want to ensure consistency in the structure of the employee information across all the databases of your company.

What You Do	How You Do It
1. Specify the database to which you want to export the table structure.	a. **Open the tblEmployees table.**
	b. In the tblEmployees table, observe that the various fields, such as EmployeeID, FirstName, LastName, and DeptCode, are displayed.
	c. In the Navigation Pane, **right-click tblEmployees and choose Export→ Access Database.**
	d. In the Export - Access Database dialog box, **click Browse.**
	e. In the File Save dialog box, **navigate to the C:\084887Data\Building a Database folder.**
	f. In the File Save dialog box, **select MyComputerInventory.accdb and click Save.**

2.	**Export the table structure.**	a.	In the Export - Access Database dialog box, **click OK.**
		b.	In the Export dialog box, in the Export Tables section, **select the Definition Only option and click OK.**
		c.	In the Export - Access Database dialog box, **click Close.**

3.	**View the new blank table with the exported structure.**	a.	From the C:\084887Data\Building a Database folder, **open the MyComputer_ inventory.accdb database.**
		b.	In the Microsoft Office Access information box, **click OK.**
		c.	In the Navigation Pane, observe that a table with the name tblEmployees is exported.
		d.	**Open the tblEmployees table.**
		e.	In the tblEmployees table, observe that only the field names, such as EmployeeID, FirstName, LastName, and DeptCode, have been exported.
		f.	**Close the database.**

TOPIC C
Manage Tables

In the previous topic, you examined the various methods of creating tables. After that, there might be instances where you want to change table properties or rename or delete a table. In this topic, you will manage tables and set their properties.

The tables you created may need to be changed over time, based on changing needs. There may be instances when the data in a table may become outdated. Also, there may be occasions wherein you would like to change table properties according to the changing design needs. Access provides a very flexible environment to modify tables, as well as set their properties and perform operations such as renaming or deleting tables. By manipulating the properties of tables, you will be able to manage tables dynamically and more efficiently.

The Table Properties Dialog Box

The Table Properties dialog box allows you to add comments about a table. It also displays additional details, such as the date the table was created and last modified. Further, it gives you options for hiding the table and enabling row level tracking, a feature that can be helpful when a database has multiple simultaneous users. When this option is selected, conflicts between users editing the same data are tracked based on the row level of a table, rather than the default column level.

Table Design Options

The Object Designers category in the Access Options dialog box is used to set the design time properties of database objects. Using this option, you can set the default design time properties of a table such as the default data type for new fields, the default size of the data type, and the default size for number values. It also allows you to specify a default primary key value for imported data. Further, you can enable the Show Property Update Options Buttons feature.

How to Manage Tables
Procedure Reference: Delete or Rename a Table

To delete or rename a table:

1. Open the desired database.
2. If desired, rename a table.
   a. In the Navigation Pane, right-click a table and choose Rename.
   b. In the text box that appears in the selected table, type the desired table name.
   c. Press Enter, or click anywhere in the Navigation Pane to deselect the table.
3. If necessary, delete a table.
   1. In the Navigation Pane, right-click a table and choose Delete.
   2. In the Microsoft Office Access warning box, click Yes to delete the selected table.

Procedure Reference: Add a Description to a Table

To add a description to a table:

1. Open the desired database.

2. In the Navigation Pane, right-click the desired table and choose Table Properties.

3. In the [Table name] Properties dialog box, in the Description text box, type the desired text.

4. Click OK to close the [Table name] Properties dialog box.

5. Right-click anywhere in the Navigation Pane and choose View By→Details to view the description under the name of the desired table.

 The Navigation Pane allows you to view the details of database objects, such as the date the object was created, the date it was last modified, and a brief description about the object (if specified).

Procedure Reference: Customize Tables Using the Access Options Dialog Box

To customize tables using the Access Options dialog box:

1. Click the Office button and then click Access Options.

2. In the Access Options dialog box, in the left pane, select Object Designers.

3. In the right pane, in the Table Design section, select the desired commands in order to change the default table design.

4. Click OK to apply the changes.

ACTIVITY 3-5

Managing Tables

Data Files:

Source.accdb

Before You Begin:

From the C:\084887Data\Building a Database folder, open the Source.accdb file.

Scenario:

You have created a database and stored data in multiple tables. You realize that the data stored in a particular table is outdated and not needed anymore. Also, you want to make the other tables easily recognizable so that you need not open them to see what type of data is stored in them.

What You Do	How You Do It
1. Delete a table.	a. In the Navigation Pane, **right-click tblNotes and choose Delete.**
	b. In the Microsoft Office Access warning box, **click Yes** to delete the tblNotes table.
	c. In the Navigation Pane, observe that the tblNotes table has been removed.
2. Rename a table.	a. In the Navigation Pane, **right-click tblEmployees and choose Rename.**
	b. Observe that a text box has been displayed in the place of the table name.
	c. In the text box, **type *tblNewEmployees***
	d. In the Navigation Pane, **click anywhere** to deselect the table.
	e. Observe that the name of the table has changed to tblNewEmployees.

3. **Add a description to a table.**

    a. In the Navigation Pane, **right-click tblComputers and choose Table Properties.**

    b. In the TblComputers Properties dialog box, in the Description text box, **type *Computer Purchase Details***

    c. **Click OK.**

    d. **Right-click anywhere in the Navigation Pane below the table names and choose View By→Details.**

    e. Observe that, under the table name tblComputers, the description is displayed in the third line.

    f. **Close the database.**

TOPIC D
Create a Table Relationship

In the previous topic, you created tables in your database to store data. Tables in a database contain related data, and several different types of relationships may exist between tables. In this topic, you will create relationships between tables in an Access database.

Before you can realize the full potential of a relational database for querying, generating reports, and updating data, you need to create the appropriate relationships between the tables of the database. For example, when you enter data in a table, there are chances that you might forget to enter the appropriate data across related tables. This may cause data inconsistency. Setting table relationships at the start will help you ensure that the correct data is stored across all related tables in the database.

Referential Integrity

Definition:

Referential integrity is a process that ensures data validity across two tables. Referential integrity is enforced by ensuring that all the corresponding values of a foreign key have a corresponding entry in the primary key field. Referential integrity disallows the entry of invalid data.

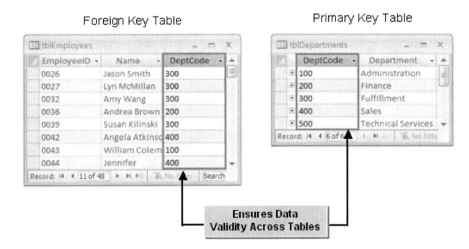

Figure 3-2: *Referential integrity ensures that every foreign key has a corresponding primary key value.*

Example:

An employee cannot belong to a department that does not exist. The Departments table contains all the existing departments. You need to ensure that all the values in the foreign key field in an Employees table match the values in the primary key field of the Departments table.

Guidelines to Enforcing Referential Integrity

Enforcing referential integrity for a relationship can avoid the loss or inadvertent updating of data.

Guidelines

You can set referential integrity between two tables if the following are true:

● Both tables are in the same Access database.

● The matching field is a primary key in one table or has a unique index.

● The related fields have the same data type (the exception is that an AutoNumber field can be related to a Number data type with a field size of Long Integer).

Example:

A CustomerID AutoNumber field in the Customers table is a unique primary key and can be related to a number field in the Orders table in a one-to-many relationship. You don't want to allow the user to enter any order data for a customer that doesn't have a record in the Customers table. Nor do you want the user to alter the CustomerID field for a record in the Customers table because that would break the link with the related orders data for that customer. Deleting a customer record that has matching order records would also not be allowed. This is a good candidate for enforcing referential integrity.

The Relationships Window

The Relationships window displays any existing relationships between various tables in a database. If no table relationships have been defined and you are opening the Relationships window for the first time, Access prompts you to add a table or query to the window.

The Edit Relationships Dialog Box

The Edit Relationships dialog box allows you to change a table relationship. Using this dialog box, you can change the tables or queries involved on either side of the relationship. It also allows you to create new relationships and specify join properties. You can also enforce referential integrity rules and cascade options.

Rule	Description
Enforce Referential Integrity	This rule ensures that you will not be able to enter a value in the foreign key table field if a corresponding value does not exist in the primary key table field.
Cascade Delete Related Records	This rule prevents you from deleting a record from a primary table if matching records exist in a related table. You need to delete records in foreign key tables before deleting them in the primary key table.
Cascade Update Related Fields	This rule prevents you from making changes to a primary key table field if matching records exist in related tables. You need to update records in foreign key tables before updating them in the primary key table.

Join Lines

A join line is drawn between two fields in different tables to indicate that the two tables are linked or joined by the data in those two fields. Each end of the join line will have either a 1 or an infinity symbol. This denotes the kind of relationship between the two tables such as one-to-one relationship or one-to-many relationship.

How to Create a Table Relationship

Procedure Reference: Create a Table Relationship

To create a table relationship:

1. On the Database Tools tab, in the Show/Hide group, click Relationships to display the Relationships window.
2. Display the Show Table dialog box.
   - On the Relationship Tools Design contextual tab, in the Relationships group, click Show Table.
   - Or, right-click anywhere in the Relationships window and choose Show Table.
3. In the Show Table dialog box, on the Tables tab, select the desired tables.
4. Click Add to add the selected tables to the Relationships window.
5. In the Show Table dialog box, click Close to close the dialog box.
6. In the Relationships window, from the desired table, drag the desired field to the matching field in the other table.
7. In the Edit Relationships dialog box, check the Enforce Referential Integrity check box to enforce referential integrity in the relationship.
8. If desired, check the Cascade Update Related Fields and Cascade Delete Related Records check boxes.
9. Click Create to establish a relationship between the two tables.

Procedure Reference: Print a Table Relationship

To print a table relationship:

1. On the Database Tools tab, in the Show/Hide group, click Relationships to display the Relationships window.
2. On the Relationship Tools Design contextual tab, in the Tools group, click Relationship Report to display the table relationship in the form of a report.
3. Save the table relationship report.
4. On the Print Preview tab, click Print.
5. If desired, set the print options.
6. In the Print dialog box, click OK to print the relationship report.

ACTIVITY 3-6
Creating a Table Relationship

Data Files:

Department.accdb

Before You Begin:

From the C:\084887Data\Building a Database folder, open the Department.accdb file.

Scenario:

You have created a database and stored all the required data in it in different tables. You want to relate these tables so you can efficiently retrieve and manipulate the required information as necessary. Also, you want to generate a report that illustrates how these tables are related.

What You Do	How You Do It
1. **Display the required tables in the Relationships window.**	a. On the Database Tools tab, in the Show/Hide group, **click Relationships** to display the Relationships window.
	b. On the Relationship Tools Design contextual tab, in the Relationships group, **click Show Table.**
	c. In the Show Table dialog box, **verify that the Tables tab is selected.**
	d. On the Tables tab, **select tblDepartments.**
	e. **Hold down Ctrl,** and on the Tables tab, **select tblNewEmployees.**
	f. **Click Add** to add all the selected tables to the Relationships window.
	g. **Click Close** to close the Show Table dialog box.

2. **Create a table relationship.**

    a. In the Relationships window, from the tblDepartments table, **drag the DeptCode field to the DeptCode field in the tblNewEmployees table.**

    b. In the Edit Relationships dialog box, **check the Enforce Referential Integrity check box** to enforce referential integrity in the relationship.

    c. **Click Create.**

    d. In the Relationships window, observe that a join line connecting the DeptCode fields in the two tables is displayed, indicating a one-to-many relationship between the two tables.

3. **Print the table relationship.**

    a. In the Tools group, **click Relationship Report.**

    b. Observe that the table relationship is displayed in the form of a report, and the Print Preview tab is displayed on the Ribbon.

    c. **Click the Office button and choose Save As.**

    d. In the Save As dialog box, **type *rptDepartment* and click OK.**

    e. On the Print Preview tab, **click Print** to display the Print dialog box.

    f. In the Print dialog box, **click OK** to print the relationship report. You can also print a relationship from the Print Preview tab.

    g. **Close the Relationships For Department report and the Relationships window.**

TOPIC E
Save a Database as a Previous Version

In the previous topic, you created tables and set relationships between them. However, you want to make your database accessible for users who do not have the 2007 version of Microsoft Office Access installed on their computers. In this topic, you will save a database as a previous version.

There can be instances where you will have to share your database with your colleagues, and not all of them may have the most recent version of Microsoft Office Access installed on their computers. In such cases, the database you share will be of no use to them, because older versions don't recognize the .accdb file format. Knowing how to save a database as a previous file format version of Access will help you to overcome this problem.

The Save As Option

The Save As option available in the Microsoft Office Button menu can be used for saving a database as different versions of Microsoft Office Access. Using this option, you can save a database as 2000, 2002–2003, and 2007 versions of Access. To save a .accdb file format to a .mdb file format, the database must not include any of the enhanced features available in Access 2007. Examples of such new features that will not work in previous versions of Access include the Attachment data type, multivalued lookup fields, and Memo field history tracking.

How to Save a Database as a Previous Version
Procedure Reference: Save a Database as a Previous Version

To save a database as a previous version:
1. Open the desired database.
2. Save the database as the desired previous version.
    - From the Office Button menu, choose Save As→Access 2002 - 2003 Database to save the database using the 2002 - 2003 file format version.
    - From the Office Button menu, choose Save As→Access 2000 Database to save the database using the 2000 file format version.
3. If necessary, in the Save As dialog box, navigate to the desired folder, and rename the file with a desired name.
4. Click Save to save the database in the version that you selected.
5. Verify that the database has been saved correctly.

ACTIVITY 3-7

Saving a Database as a Previous Version

Before You Begin:
From the C:\084887Data\Building a Database folder, open the Department.accdb file.

Scenario:
You need to distribute a copy of the database to all employees in your organization. You are not sure that all employees have the 2007 version of Access installed on their workstations. You want to ensure that every employee is able to open the database even if he or she is working with a previous version of Access.

What You Do	How You Do It
1. Save the database in the 2002 - 2003 version.	a. From the Office Button menu, **choose Save As→Access 2002 - 2003 Database.**
	b. If necessary, in the Save As dialog box, **navigate to the C:\084887Data\Building a Database folder.**
	c. In the Save As dialog box, **rename the file to *MyDepartment2002–2003*.**
	d. In the Save As Type drop-down list, observe that Microsoft Access Database (2002–2003) (*.mdb) is selected.
	e. **Click Save** to save the database in the 2002-2003 version.
	f. On the title bar, observe that the file format displayed is Access 2002 - 2003.

2. **Save the database in the 2000 version.**

a. From the Office Button menu, **choose Save As→Access 2000 Database.**

b. In the Save As dialog box, **rename the file to *MyDepartment2000*.**

c. In the Save As Type drop-down list, observe that Microsoft Access Database (2000) (*.mdb) is selected.

d. **Click Save** to save the database in the 2000 version.

e. On the title bar, observe that the file format displayed is Access 2000.

f. **Close the database.**

Lesson 3 Follow-up

In this lesson, you implemented your database design plan. When appropriate, using an existing template for a table—or for even a template for an entire database—can save you time and trouble. But building a database from scratch gives you more flexibility.

1. **Under what circumstances would you prefer to create a database using a template over creating one from scratch?**

2. **What do you think are the factors that need to be taken into account when determining the data types of table fields?**

4 Managing Data in a Table

Lesson Time: 35 minutes

Lesson Objectives:

In this lesson, you will manage data in a table.

You will:

- Modify data in a table.
- Sort records in a table.
- Work with subdatasheets.

Introduction

You have designed a database, created tables, and populated them with data. However, a database is never static. You will need to manage and update tables to keep data current. In this lesson, you will manage data in a table.

Databases form the basis for managing data in a company. Therefore, it is important to continuously manage them by making updates to the database tables and maintaining data integrity. Knowing how to work with data in a table will allow you to manage data in your database with ease.

TOPIC A
Modify Table Data

You have created tables in an Access database. To keep data in these tables current, you need to know how to add, delete, and update data in a table. In this topic, you will modify data in an existing table.

Information in a database is subject to change. Tools that help update information frequently and easily are vital to efficiently maintaining your databases. Knowing how to use these tools allows you to modify and update data in tables.

The Find Command

The Find command helps you to quickly locate specific data. The Find tab in the Find And Replace dialog box has various find options that will help you search data by specifying a criterion.

Option	Used To
Find What text box	Specify the text to be located.
Look In drop-down list	Specify that the search target should include either the column or the entire table.
Match drop-down list	Restrict the scope of the search.
Search drop-down list	Specify the direction in which the search should proceed.
Match Case check box	Specify that the search has to be for the characters with the same casing specified in the Find What text box.
Search Fields As Formatted check box	Search field values with the input mask. The check box is automatically checked when an input mask format is set for a table. Unchecking this check box will lead to improper results or no results for a search operation.
Find Next button	Locate the next instance of the search criteria.
Cancel button	Stop the search and close the Find And Replace dialog box.

The Replace Command

The Replace command helps you to replace the existing data within a database with new data. The Replace tab in the Find And Replace dialog box contains replace options that help you replace data.

Option	Used To
The Replace With text box	Specify the text with which the located data should be replaced.
The Replace button	Replace the selected instance of the search criteria.
The Replace All button	Replace every instance of the search criteria with the new data.

The Totals Feature

Using the *Totals* feature, you can add a Total row to your table. It provides commands for summation, average, count of records, maximum, minimum, standard deviation, and variance of the entries in a column.

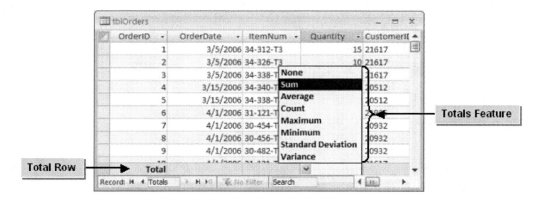

Figure 4-1: A Total row.

How to Modify Table Data

Procedure Reference: Modify Data in a Table

To modify data in a table:

1. In the desired table, insert a new record.
   - On the Home tab, in the Records group, click New and enter the new record data.
   - Or, click the last value of the last record and press Enter to create a new record and enter the new record data.
2. Update data in a record.
   a. Select the desired field.
   b. Type the appropriate value to update the record.
3. If necessary, delete a selected record.
   - In the Records group, from the Delete drop-down list, select Delete Record and click Yes.
   - Right-click the selected record, choose Delete Record and click Yes.
   - Or, press Delete and click Yes.
4. Save the table.

Procedure Reference: Find and Replace Data in a Record

To find and replace data in a record:

1. Open the desired table.
2. Open the Find And Replace dialog box.
   - On the Home tab, in the Find group, click Find to open the Find And Replace dialog box.
   - Or, press Ctrl+F.
3. On the Find tab, in the Find What text box, type the text you want to find.
4. If necessary, set the search options in the Find And Replace dialog box.
5. Click Find Next to find text matching the text in the Find What text box.
6. If desired, replace data in a record.
   a. On the Replace tab, in the Find What text box, type the text you want to replace.
   b. If necessary, set the search options.
   c. In the Replace With text box, type the text that you want to replace the existing text with.
   d. Replace the found text with the text specified in the Replace With text box.
      - Click Replace to replace the selected instance of the search criteria.
      - Click Replace All to replace every instance of the search criteria with the new text.
7. In the Find And Replace dialog box, click the Close button.

Procedure Reference: Add the Total Row to a Table

To add the Total row to a table:

1. Open the desired table and, on the Home tab, in the Records group, click Totals to add a Total row at the end of the table.

2. In the Total row, click in the field under the column that you need to total and select the desired option. The options include Sum, Average, Count, Standard Deviation, Variance, Maximum, and Minimum.

3. Save the table.

ACTIVITY 4-1

Modifying Records in a Table

Data Files:

Sample Tables.accdb

Before You Begin:

From the C:\084887Data\Managing Data in a Table folder, open the Sample Tables.accdb file, and open the tblEmployees table.

Scenario:

You are part of the office administrative staff, and modifying and updating records are part of your daily routine. Due to a new Human Resources Department initiative, many job titles have been revised. You want to make sure that the titles of employees designated as Sales Representatives are changed to Sales Executives.

What You Do	How You Do It
1. **Add a new employee record to the table.**	a. On the Home tab, in the Records group, **click New.**
	b. In the EmployeeID field, **type *0143* and press Tab.**
	c. In the LastName field, **type *Bernstein* and press Tab.**
	d. **Enter the data in the following fields.** • FirstName : Edward • Address : 127 Larkspur Lane • City : Potter • State : OH • ZipCode : 72057 • HomePhone : 5095553254 • DeptNum : 400 • HireDate : 8/12/1999 • Title : Human Resources Benefits Specialist

2.	**Find a record with "Sales Representative".**	a.	In the Find group, **click Find** to display the Find And Replace dialog box.
		b.	On the Find tab, in the Find What text box, **type *Sales Representative***
		c.	From the Look In drop-down list, **select tblEmployees.**
		d.	**Click Find Next** to locate the first record containing the text "Sales Representative".
3.	**Replace all instances of "Sales Representative" with "Sales Executive".**	a.	**Select the Replace tab.**
		b.	On the Replace tab, in the Replace With text box, **type *Sales Executive***
		c.	**Click Replace All.**
		d.	In the Microsoft Office Access warning box, **click Yes.**
		e.	In the Find And Replace dialog box, **click the Close button.**
4.	**Update an employee record.**	a.	**Scroll to the left** to view the record with the EmployeeID of 0051.
		b.	If necessary, **scroll to the right** to view the HomePhone value of the record with the EmployeeID value of 0051.
		c.	In the HomePhone value of the record with the EmployeeID value of 0051 and HomePhone value of (509) 555-5011, **double-click 5011** to select the last four digits of the phone number.
		d.	**Type *5267***
		e.	If necessary, **Scroll to the left** to view the EmployeeID column.

5. **Delete an employee record from the table.**

   a. **Scroll to the top** to view EmployeeID 0026.

   b. **Move the mouse pointer to before the EmployeeID column in the row with the EmployeeID value of 0026** and, when it changes to an arrow, **click** to select the row.

   c. In the Records group, from the Delete drop-down list, **select Delete Record.**

   d. In the Microsoft Office Access warning box, **click Yes.**

   e. Observe that the record with the EmployeeID value of 0026 is no longer included in the table.

   f. **Close the table.**

6. **Add a Total row to the table.**

   a. **Open the tblOrders table.**

   b. In the Records group, **click Totals.**

   c. In the Total row, **click in the field corresponding to Quantity** and, from the drop-down list, **select Sum.**

   d. Observe that the result displayed is 805, which is the sum of all values in the Quantity column.

   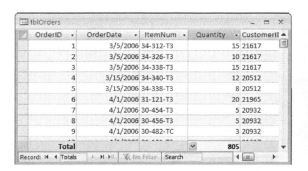

   e. **Save and close the table.**

   f. **Close the database.**

TOPIC B

Pg 4 used
109 - 117

Sort Records

In the previous topic, you modified the data in a table. In a large table, retrieving records that need to be modified, or analyzing data, may be difficult without knowing the tools that enable you to sort information in a table. In this topic, you will sort records in a table.

It is difficult to find a specific group of data in a database with a number of large tables. Organizing data in a specific order, such as by ascending or descending order of values, can help sort needed information in a database. To simplify the process and reduce the time you spend searching for data, Access provides several techniques that will assist you in sorting and locating the desired records.

Sorting Records

Definition:

A *sort* is a method of viewing data by arranging it in a specific order. Data can be sorted in either *ascending order* or *descending order*, based on numeric or alphabetic information.

Example:

A table is sorted in ascending order in the following example.

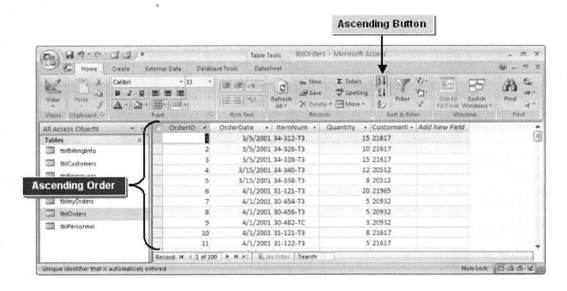

Figure 4-2: A table in ascending order.

Sorting Records According to Multiple Fields

Access allows you to sort records according to two or more fields simultaneously. The fields are arranged so that they are adjacent, and the first field selected is considered the primary sort field and the others are considered the secondary sort field(s). This means that the records will be arranged in the desired order according to the primary field first. For records with identical values in that field, the secondary fields will be used to determine the sort order for those records.

How to Sort Records

Procedure Reference: Sort Records in a Table According to a Single Field

To sort records in a table according to a single field:

1. In the desired table, select the field by which you need to sort the table.
2. Sort the table.
    *   Sort the table in ascending order.
        *   On the Home tab, in the Sort & Filter group, click the Ascending button.
        *   Or, in the table header of the desired field, from the drop-down list, select Sort A To Z.
    *   Sort the table in descending order.
        *   On the Home tab, in the Sort & Filter group, click the Descending button.
        *   Or, in the table header of the desired field, from the drop-down list, select Sort Z To A.
3. If necessary, in the Sort & Filter group, click the Clear All Sorts button to restore the records to the original order.

Procedure Reference: Sort Records in a Table According to Two or More Fields

To sort records in a table according to two or more fields:

1. In the desired table, rearrange the columns in the table so that the desired sort fields are next to each other.
2. Select the field that will be the primary sort field and then select one or more fields that will be the secondary sort field(s).
3. Sort the table.
4. If necessary, in the Sort & Filter group, click the Clear All Sorts button to restore the records to the original order.

ACTIVITY 4-2

Sorting Records in a Table

Data Files:

Sort Tables.accdb

Before You Begin:

From the C:\084887Data\Managing Data in a Table folder, open the Sort Tables.accdb file.

Scenario:

Your sales manager would like to know how many orders in the tblCustomers table have been placed by Zilinski's Home Store, and how many have been placed by Household Helper.

What You Do	How You Do It
1. Observe the CustomerID numbers for Household Helper and Zilinski's Home Store.	a. **Open the tblCustomers table.** b. Observe the Household Helper record and note that the CustomerID number is the lowest in the table, and observe the Zilinski's Home Store record and note that the CustomerID number is the highest in the table. c. **Close the table.**
2. Sort the tblOrders table in ascending order, thereby displaying Household Helper orders at the top of the table.	a. **Open the tblOrders table.** b. If necessary, **expand the CustomerID column.** c. **Click in the first field in the CustomerID column.** d. On the Home tab, in the Sort & Filter group, **click the Ascending button.** e. Observe that there are three orders with a CustomerID value of 20151 at the top of the list that correspond to the three Household Helper orders.

3.	**Sort the table in descending order, displaying Zilinski's orders at the top of the table.**	a.	In the Sort & Filter group, **click the Descending button.**
		b.	Observe that there are 10 orders with a CustomerID value of 21965 at the top of the list that correspond to the 10 Zilinski's Home Store orders.
4.	**Clear all sorts in the table.**	a.	In the Sort & Filter group, **click the Clear All Sorts button.**
		b.	Observe that the table is restored to its original state.
		c.	**Close the table.**
		d.	In the Microsoft Office Access warning box, **click No** to close the table without saving the changes.
		e.	**Close the database.**

TOPIC C
Work with Subdatasheets

In the previous topic, you sorted data within a table. But sometimes, you may need to view data from a table while working on another, related table. In this topic, you will work with subdatasheets.

Understanding and knowing how Access tables are related and evaluating the relationships between them is a great starting point in building a database. But, if you are working with a table and need to view the data in another related table, how can you display it? The Subdatasheet feature allows you to view related data for any selected record.

Subdatasheets

Definition:

A *subdatasheet* is a datasheet that is nested within another datasheet that contains data related to the first datasheet. When a record has a subdatasheet, it is indicated by a plus sign (+) in the left column. When you click the plus sign, the subdatasheet is displayed and the relevant data in the related table is displayed.

Example:

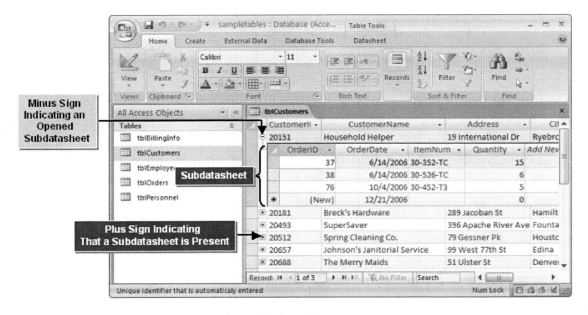

Figure 4-3: *A table with a subdatasheet displayed.*

How to Modify Subdatasheets

Procedure Reference: View or Modify Data in Subdatasheets

To view or modify data in a subdatasheet:

1. Open the desired table with the subdatasheet.

2. Click the plus sign (+) to the left of the record you need to view to expand the subdatasheet and view the related data.

3. Select the field and type the desired value to modify the data.

4. If necessary, click the minus sign (−) to the left of the record to collapse the subdatasheet.

ACTIVITY 4-3

Modifying Data in a Subdatasheet

Data Files:

Subdatasheet.accdb

Before You Begin:

From the C:\084887Data\Managing Data in a Table folder, open the Subdatasheet.accdb file.

Scenario:

You want to retrieve the order details of various customers and send invoices to various companies that have placed orders with your company. The only information you've been given is the customer ID. The information you need is in theCustomers table. Also, you have been asked to change the quantity entry from 10 to 13 for OrderID 15 for Merry Maids.

What You Do	How You Do It
1. **Observe the number of orders placed by the customer.**	a. **Open the tblCustomers table.**
	b. If necessary, **expand the CustomerID column.**
	c. Observe that the field with CustomerID 20151 is selected.
	d. To the left of CustomerID 20151, **click the plus sign (+)** to expand the subdatasheet.
	e. Observe that the plus sign (+) changes to a minus sign (-), indicating that the subdatasheet is expanded with three orders listed for the OrderID.

	f. To the left of CustomerID 20151, **click the minus sign (-)** to collapse the subdatasheet.

2. In the tblCustomers table, **expand the subdatasheets for CustomerIDs 20493 and 20688.**

   a. **Click the plus sign (+) in the left column of the record with the CustomerID value of 20493** to display the subdatasheet.

   b. **Click the plus sign (+) in the left column of the record with the CustomerID value of 20688** to display the subdatasheet.

   c. Observe that both subdatasheets you have opened can remain open at the same time.

3. **Change the quantity entry from 10 to 13 for OrderID 15 for Merry Maids.**

   a. In the subdatasheet for CustomerID 20688, **double-click the Quantity value of the record that has the OrderID of 15 and type *13*.**

   b. **Press Tab.**

   c. In the Quick Access toolbar, **click Save** and in the Microsoft Office Access warning box, **click Yes** to save the changes and **close the table.**

   d. **Close the database.**

Lesson 4 Follow-up

In this lesson, you added, deleted, and updated data in a table. Updating data in tables will provide reliable, up-to-date information and also prevent the database from becoming outdated.

1. **How helpful can the sort options be when you update records in a large table of your database?**

2. **What are the instances when you will use the Find and Replace commands while managing databases?**

Don't do 120 -123

5 | Querying a Database

Lesson Time: 1 hour(s), 10 minutes

Lesson Objectives:

In this lesson, you will query a database using different methods.

You will:

● Filter records based on a search criterion.

● Create a query.

● Add criteria to a query.

● Add a calculated field to a query.

● Perform calculations on a record grouping.

Introduction

In the previous lesson, you performed some preliminary data retrieval tasks, such as searching for and replacing specific values in a table and sorting table data. But you may need to perform more complex tasks such as retrieving records that meet certain criteria. In this lesson, you will create queries and filter data.

Unless you have a mechanism for isolating and extracting data, looking for specific information in a database will be like looking for a needle in a haystack. A database is helpful only when you can retrieve data as easily as you can add it to the database. Knowing how to work with queries will greatly reduce the time it takes to retrieve data from a database.

TOPIC A
Filter Records

You sorted the records in a table to arrange them more meaningfully. But if you need to retrieve a subset of data from a table, you can use the filter options. In this topic, you will filter records in a table.

Database tables usually store broad categories of information from which you may need to cull out specific subsets of data. For example, in a table that lists employee details, if you are trying to obtain a list of employees in the Human Resource department, it would be tedious to use the Find option or to manually check each employee's department or designation. The filter options in Access allow you to filter records by any column of the table.

The Filter Feature

Using the filter feature, you can filter data to display only the records that match your criteria. In Access 2007, you can *filter* data based on the values in a column. You can apply filters such as text filters for the text data type, number filters for the number data type, and date filters for the date data type. When you apply a filter to a column that is already filtered, the existing filter is removed. However, it's possible to specify different filters for each field displayed in the table; that is, multiple filters can be applied to a table at the same time.

Filtering Techniques

The Sort & Filter group has three options—the Selection drop-down list, the Advanced drop-down list, and the Toggle Filter button—that allow you to filter the records in a table.

Option	Description
	The options in the Selection drop-down list allow you to filter items depending on the value of the selected field. If you want to filter by a date field, the Selection drop-down list includes options for selecting dates before or after a specific date or even items within a range of dates.
	The Advanced drop-down list has options that allow you to filter multiple fields in a form, apply filters that are not commonly available in the filter list, or save your filter as an actual query object in the database.
	The Toggle Filter button is used to move between the filtered view and the unfiltered view of data in the table.

How to Filter Records

Procedure Reference: Filter Records in a Table

To filter records in a table:

1. Open the desired table and select the column that the data is to be filtered by.
2. On the Home tab, in the Sort & Filter group, click Filter.
3. On the context menu that is displayed, uncheck the check boxes that are not required and click OK.

Procedure Reference: Save the Filter as a Query

To save the filter as a query:

1. Open the desired table and filter the records in the table.
2. Click the Office button and choose Save As to display the Save As dialog box.
3. In the Save As dialog box, in the Save [TableName] To text box, type the desired name for the query.
4. From the As drop-down list, select Query and click OK.
5. In the Microsoft Office Access warning box, click Yes.

Procedure Reference: Remove a Filter

To remove a filter:

1. Select the column in which you want to remove the filter.
2. Remove the filter to display all items in the table.
   - Remove the filter using the context menu.
     a. On the Home tab, in the Sort & Filter group, click Filter.
     b. On the context menu that is displayed, check the (Select All) check box.
     c. Click OK.
   - Click Filter and, on the context menu, choose Clear Filter From [Column Name].
   - On the Home tab, in the Sort & Filter group, click Toggle Filter.
   - Or, on the Record Navigation bar, click the Filtered button.

ACTIVITY 5-1
Filtering Records

Data Files:

Gourmet Shop.accdb

Before You Begin:

From the C:\084887Data\Querying a Database folder, open the Gourmet Shop.accdb file.

Scenario:

You are the delivery manager of a gourmet shop. While taking stock of the store products, you find that the supplies of blackberry preserves are low, so you need to identify the quantity of blackberry preserves needed to meet current orders. You will analyze the records and identify the amount of blackberry preserves currently available.

What You Do	How You Do It
1. **Obtain the product ID of blackberry preserves.**	a. **Open the tblProducts table.**
	b. If necessary, **expand the ProductID column.**
	c. Observe that the product ID corresponding to Blackberry Preserves is 3.
	d. **Close the tblProducts table without saving changes.**
2. **Filter the orders placed for blackberry preserves.**	a. **Open the tblOrderDetails table and click the ProductID column header.**
	b. On the Home tab, in the Sort & Filter group, **click Filter.**
	c. On the context menu that is displayed, **uncheck the (Select All) check box.**
	d. **Check the 3 check box and click OK.**
	e. Observe that only the rows with the product ID of 3 are displayed.

3.	**Count the number of orders placed for blackberry preserves.**	a.	In the Records group, **click Totals** to add a Total row.
		b.	In the Total row, **click in the cell corresponding to Quantity** to display a drop-down list.
		c.	From the drop-down list, **select Sum** to view the number of orders placed for blackberry preserves, which is 866.
4.	**Save the filter as the *qryOrders* query.**	a.	**Click the Office button and choose Save As.**
		b.	In the Save As dialog box, in the Save 'TblOrderDetails' To text box, **type *qryOrders***
		c.	From the As drop-down list, **select Query and click OK.**
		d.	In the Microsoft Office Access warning box, **click Yes.**
		e.	**Close the qryOrders query document window.**
5.	**Remove the filter.**	a.	**Click the ProductID column header.**
		b.	On the Record Navigation bar, **click the Filtered button**  to remove the filter.
		c.	Observe that the total changes to 7895, indicating that the filter is removed and all the records are listed.
		d.	**Click Save** to retain memory of this filter in the table for future use by using the Toggle Filter button.
		e.	**Close the table and then close the database.**

Microsoft® Office Access™ 2007: Level 1 (Second Edition)

TOPIC B
Create a Query

Filtering allows you to select data within a table, but often you may need to select data from multiple tables. Queries allow you to retrieve data from related tables. In this topic, you will create queries.

There may be instances where you need to retrieve relevant information from different tables at the same time; for instance, you may have to identify employees who come under a specific department and analyze their payroll from the database. You can retrieve such information by creating queries, which allow you to retrieve data from multiple tables. You can also save and store the queries as reusable Access objects.

The Query Wizard

Using the *Query Wizard*, you can create a simple query. The wizard guides you through a series of steps to help you design a query. In the wizard, you can select the desired tables and fields that you want to include in the query. The output of the Query Wizard will be displayed as a query object in the Navigation Pane.

Types of Queries

You can create several types of queries using the Query Wizard.

Query	Enables You To
Simple	Select fields from multiple tables and queries.
Crosstab	Calculate aggregates such as sum, average, and count, and group them.
Find Duplicates	Find duplicate field values.
Find Unmatched	Find records in a table with no related records in another table.

The Query Design Feature

The *Query Design feature* enables you to design a query. There are several groups on the Design contextual tab that allow you to design queries.

Group	Enables You To
Results	Change the view and execute a query.
Query Type	Specify the query types that can be used to select, append, update, or delete records. It also has SQL-specific options and an option for creating a crosstab query.
Query Setup	Insert and delete rows and columns, build expressions, and set up a query from a table, another query, or both.

124   Lesson 5: Querying a Database

Group	Enables You To
Show/Hide	Show or hide tables, the total, the Property Sheet pane, and query parameters.

Query Object Views

The query object can be accessed using different views in Access. The views available are Design View, SQL View, Datasheet View, PivotTable View, and PivotChart View. Each of these views contains tabs through which you can manipulate the query object.

The Show Table Dialog Box

The Show Table dialog box displays the tables and queries in the database, allowing you to add multiple tables and queries to the Design view to create a new query. The Tables, Queries, and Both tabs in the Show Table dialog box list only the tables, or only the queries, or both queries and tables in the database, respectively.

How to Create a Query

Procedure Reference: Create a Select Query Using the Query Design Feature

To create a query using the Query Design feature:

1. In the desired database, on the Create tab, in the Other group, click Query Design to open the Show Table dialog box.
2. In the Show Table dialog box, select the tables or queries to be used for the query.
    - Select the Tables tab to view the list of tables in the database.
    - Select the Queries tab to view the list of queries in the database.
    - Select the Both tab to view a consolidated list of both tables and queries in the database.
3. For each desired table or query, select the element and click Add to add the database element to the Design view and then click Close to close the dialog box.
4. On the Design contextual tab, click Select to create a Select query.
5. In the query window, in the list box, double-click the required fields to add them to the query design grid.
6. Save the query.
7. Run the query.
    - On the Design contextual tab, in the Results group, click Run.
    - Or, in the Navigation Pane, double-click the query to run it.

Procedure Reference: Create a Select Query Using the Query Wizard

To create a query using the Query Wizard:

1. In the desired database, on the Create tab, in the Other group, click Query Wizard to display the New Query dialog box.
2. In the New Query dialog box, select Simple Query Wizard and click OK to open the Simple Query Wizard.

3. In the Simple Query Wizard, from the Tables/Queries drop-down list, select the table that contains the fields you desire for your query.

4. In the Available Fields list box, double-click the fields to add them to the Selected Fields list box and click Next.

5. Repeat steps 3 and 4 as necessary to add fields from other tables and queries.

6. Select the type of query and click Next.

7. Save the query, select if you would like to open the query or modify the design, and click Finish to close the wizard and execute the query.

Trust Center

Access 2007 does not allow the query to execute if the database is not placed in a trusted location. To enable the Trust Center Settings, in the Access Options dialog box, in the Trust Center category, click Trust Center Settings. In the Trust Center dialog box, in the Trusted Locations category, click Add New Location. In the Microsoft Office Trusted Location dialog box, specify the desired location. If necessary, check the Subfolders Of This Location Are Also Trusted check box, and then click OK. In the Trust Center dialog box, click OK. In the Access Options dialog box, click OK.

ACTIVITY 5-2
Creating a Query

Data Files:

Personnelbiz.accdb

Before You Begin:

From the C:\084887Data\Querying a Database folder, open the Personnelbiz.accdb file.

Scenario:

You want to analyze the post-appraisal pay and benefits of your team members, but the database has many other details and you are unable to locate the exact information you want. You decide to create a summarized datasheet that comprises just the fields you require.

What You Do	How You Do It
1. **Create a query.**	a. On the Create tab, in the Other group, **click Query Design.**
	b. In the Show Table dialog box, on the Tables tab, **verify that Employees is selected. Click Add and then click Close.**
	c. On the Design contextual tab, in the Query Type group, **verify that the Select query type is selected.**
	d. In the Query1 query window, in the Employees field list, **double-click EmpID** to add it to the query design grid.
	e. **Similarly, add the following fields to the query design grid:** • FirstName • LastName • Hours • PayRate
	f. On the Quick Access toolbar, **click Save.**
	g. In the Query Name text box, **type *qryPayAndBenefits* and click OK.**
	h. Notice that the query is displayed in the Navigation Pane.

2. **Execute the query and then close the query document window and database.**

   a. In the Navigation Pane, **double-click qryPayAndBenefits** to run the query.

   b. In the datasheet window, **verify that all the desired data has been included.**

   c. **Close the query window.**

   d. **Close the database.**

ACTIVITY 5-3

Creating a Select Query Using the Query Wizard

Data Files:

Select Queries.accdb

Before You Begin:

From the C:\084887Data\Querying a Database folder, open the Select Queries.accdb file.

Scenario:

You want to produce the details about the computers in your department to the Information Audit department. The details include the asset tag, manufacturer, date received, and purchase price. You find that the information you require is spread across two tables. You need to create a query to locate and display the required data.

What You Do	How You Do It
1. Launch the Query Wizard and add the Asset Tag, Date Received, and Purchase Price fields from the tblComputers table to the query.	a. On the Create tab, in the Other group, **click Query Wizard** to open the New Query dialog box.
	b. In the New Query dialog box, **verify that the Simple Query Wizard is selected and then click OK.**
	c. From the Tables/Queries drop-down list, **scroll up and select Table: tblComputers.**
	d. In the Available Fields list box, **double-click AssetTag** to add the AssetTag field to the Selected Fields list box.
	e. Similarly, **add the DateReceived and PurchasePrice fields to the query.**
2. Add the Manufacturer field in the tblManufacturers table to the query.	a. From the Tables/Queries drop-down list, **select Table: tblManufacturers.**
	b. In the Available Fields list box, **double-click Manufacturer and click Next.**
	c. **Verify that the Detail (Shows Every Field Of Every Record) option is selected and click Next.**

3. **Save the query as *qryComputers*.**

   a. In the What Title Do You Want For Your Query text box, **select the default title.**

   b. **Type *qryComputers***

   c. Under the Do You Want To Open The Query Or Modify The Query's Design section, **verify that the Open The Query To View Information option is selected and then click Finish.**

   d. Observe that the qryComputers query with the desired fields is displayed.

   e. **Close the query document window.**

   f. **Close the database.**

TOPIC C
Add Criteria to a Query

In the previous topic, you saw the need to use queries when working with multiple tables. You can also use queries to locate items in a table or across multiple tables that satisfy specific criteria. In this topic, you will add criteria to a query using the conditional and comparison operators.

Let's say you have been asked to locate all records with an hourly rate of pay exceeding a specific amount. You know the information is in the database and a query is the tool you need to extract it, but how do you do it? By incorporating conditional and comparison operators into your query, you'll be able to efficiently access this information.

Query Criteria

Definition:

A *query criterion* is a search condition used in a query to retrieve or manipulate specific information. More than one criterion can be included in a query. The query criteria are used to compare the information in the columns to a specific value. Calculations can also be performed on numeric columns before comparing information.

Example:

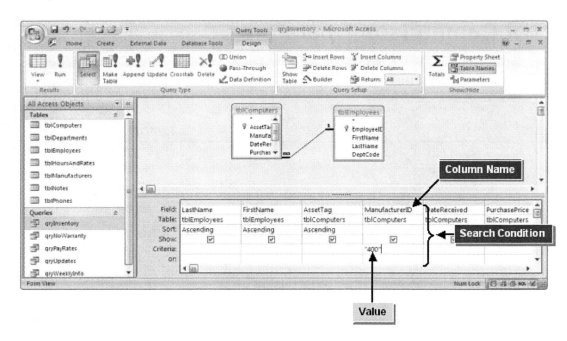

Figure 5-1: An example of a query criterion.

Comparison Operators

Definition:

Comparison operators are symbols used to compare two values. Comparison operators, when set in a criterion, establish results after comparing two or more values. The output of a comparison operator is either true or false.

Example:

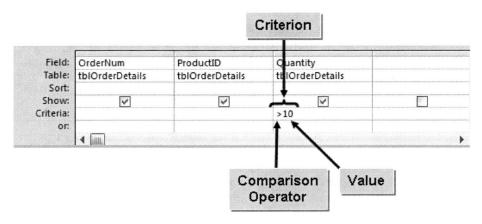

Figure 5-2: An example of a comparison operator.

List of Comparison Operators

Access supports different kinds of comparison operators. The following table summarizes the comparison operators.

Operator	Value	Example
=	Equals	= 11/29/2004
<	Less than	< K
<=	Less than or equal to	<= 2500
>	Greater than	> K
>=	Greater than or equal to	>= 2500
<>	Not equal to	<> Michigan
Between And	Within a range	Between 5/1/2005 And 8/31/2005
Is Null	Null values	Is Null

 Simply using "Null" instead of "Is Null" will also work.

Conditional Operators

Definition:

Conditional operators are operators that test for the truth of a condition. Conditional operators, such as comparison operators, return a value of either true or false. Parentheses can be used to change the order of evaluation, and the operators within parentheses are evaluated first. Conditional operators are also referred to as logical operators.

Example:

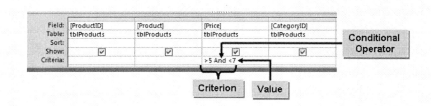

Figure 5-3: An example of a conditional operator.

List of Conditional Operators

There are three conditional operators used in Access.

Operator	Description
AND	True if both conditions are true. Example: > 5 AND <> 100
OR	True if either condition is true. Example: < 5 OR > 500
NOT	True if the single instance is not true. Example: NOT Between 100 And 200

Examples of Conditional Operators

The Access query grid provides multiple rows in which you can identify records that need to be displayed in the result set. For example, if you wanted to select all the records where a Price field is greater than $100, you could type >100 in the criteria row that is below the Price field. Using ANDs and ORs would allow you to expand or narrow the search. If you want to select all the records where the Price field is greater than $100 AND where the location of the sale is the State of California, you would add the word California to the criteria row below the State field. Both criteria should be placed on the same line. This automatically creates an AND condition. An AND condition narrows the search, and the records that are selected must meet all the criteria in order to be returned.

Putting criteria on a different line creates an OR condition, which expands the search. Using the previous example, if you were to move the word California down one row and then across, from the word or to the left of the grid area, the query would return all the records where the Price field is greater than $100 as well as all records where the State field is equal to California.

AND and OR criteria may also be typed directly in the same cell. For example, one could type California or Michigan in a state criteria row, to return all records from either state. Typing California and Michigan in a state criteria row would return no records because the value in the State field cannot be equal to both.

How to Add Criteria to a Query

Procedure Reference: Add Criteria to a Query

To add criteria:

1. Open the desired query and switch to Design view.
2. In the design grid, include the field or fields for which you want to set criteria.
3. Set the criteria.

    ● To create an AND or OR condition on a single field, include the appropriate word in the Criteria row.

    ● To create an AND condition on more than one field, enter the other criteria in the Criteria row.

    ● If desired, to create an OR condition on more than one field, enter the other criteria in the Or row.

ACTIVITY 5-4

Adding Criteria to a Query

Data Files:

Queries.accdb

Before You Begin:

From the C:\084887Data\Querying a Database folder, open the Queries.accdb file.

Scenario:

You require specific information, such as order details, including the manufacturer and the purchase price, which are crucial statistics needed to support your enterprise from time to time. In particular, you need to search in the Queries database for computers that meet specific price, department code, or manufacturer criteria.

What You Do	How You Do It
1. **Run the qryInventory query to find the computers with a purchase price over $2,000.**	a. In the Navigation Pane, **double-click qryInventory** to run the query.
	b. **Switch to Design view.**
	c. In the design grid, **scroll to the right** to view the PurchasePrice field.
	d. In the PurchasePrice field, **click in the Criteria row and type** *>2000*
	e. On the Design contextual tab, in the Results group, **click Run** to run the query.
	f. Observe that six records are returned by the query.
	g. **Scroll to the right and verify that all six records have a PurchasePrice value that is greater than 2000.**

2. Remove the PurchasePrice criteria and set the DeptCode equal to 500, and then run the query.

   a. **Switch to Design view.**

   b. In the Criteria row for the PurchasePrice field, **delete >2000.**

   c. In the design grid, **scroll to the left** to view the DeptCode field.

   d. **Click in the Criteria row for the DeptCode field and type *500* and then uncheck the Show check box for the DeptCode field.**

   e. **Run the query.**

   f. Observe that five records satisfy the condition and that you can set a criterion on a field that will not be displayed in Datasheet view.

3. Add Atlas to the criteria of the Manufacturer field.

   a. **Switch to Design view.**

   b. In the Show row, **check the check box for the DeptCode field.**

   c. In the design grid, **scroll to the right** to view the Manufacturer field.

   d. **Click in the Criteria row for the Manufacturer field and type *Atlas***

   e. **Run the query.**

   f. Observe that two records satisfy both conditions specified in the DeptCode and Manufacturer fields.

4. Delete the existing condition in the Criteria row of the Manufacturer field, and in the Or row, enter the manufacturer name *Cyber.*

   a. **Switch to Design view.**

   b. In the Criteria row for the Manufacturer field, **delete "Atlas".**

   c. In the Manufacturer field, **click in the Or row and type *Cyber***

   d. **Run the query.**

   e. Observe that the ten records that satisfy either the DeptCode field criterion or the Manufacturer field criterion are displayed.

5. Use the Between operator to create the criteria to determine how many computers were acquired during the first quarter of 2006.

a. **Switch to Design view.**

b. In the Or row for the Manufacturer field, **delete "Cyber".**

c. In the design grid, **scroll to the left** to view the DeptCode field.

d. In the Criteria row for the DeptCode field, **delete "500".**

e. In the design grid, **scroll to the right** to view the DateReceived field.

f. **Click in the Criteria row for the DateReceived field and type** *Between 1/1/2006 And 3/31/2006*

g. **Run the query.**

h. Observe that there are six records with dates that fall between 1/1/2006 and 3/31/2006.

---

6. Use the Null operator to create a criterion in the tblComputers table to locate records with a blank value, and save the query.

a. **Switch to Design view.**

b. In the design window displaying table relationships, **right-click the tblManufacturers table and select Remove Table.**

c. In the design window displaying table relationships, **right-click the tblDepartments table and choose Remove Table.**

d. In the design grid, in the DateReceived field, **delete the criteria.**

e. In the Criteria row for the ManufacturerID field, **click and type** *Is Null*

f. **Run the query.**

g. Observe that three records that satisfy this criterion are displayed. They each lack a value for the ManufacturerID field.

h. **Save and close the query and then close the database.**

TOPIC D
Add a Calculated Field to a Query

The ability to use Access conditional and comparison operators has greatly expanded your querying capacity. But you can do more by using the values in a record to produce new data that is not in the record itself. In this topic, you will add a calculated field to a query.

Imagine that your company's payroll department wants you to calculate the weekly salary for an individual who is paid by the hour. By including a calculated field that uses the employee's hourly rate, this is easily accomplished. Using a calculated field, you can display the results of the calculation as the output of the query.

The Calculated Field

A calculated field is a resultant field that derives its values from calculations performed on other fields. Unlike other fields in a table, the calculated field is not entered by the user. The value of a calculated field will change each time the expression changes.

Arithmetic Operators

Definition:

Arithmetic operators are symbols that are used to perform mathematical operations. They either add, subtract, multiply, or divide values.

Example:

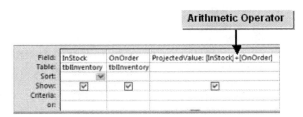

Figure 5-4: An example of an arithmetic operator.

List of Arithmetic Operators

The following table summarizes the arithmetic operators.

Arithmetic Operator	Description	Example	Result
+	Addition	value1 + value2	Value1 is added to value2
-	Subtraction	value1 - value2	Value2 is subtracted from value1
*	Multiplication	value1 * value2	Value1 is multiplied by value2
/	Division	value1 / value2	Value1 is divided by value2

Expressions

Definition:

Expressions are combinations of functions, field names, numbers, text, and operators that allow you to perform calculations to produce results. They are used to create calculated fields. Arithmetic expressions consist of table data and the arithmetic operators such as addition (+), subtraction (-), multiplication (*), and division (/). If a portion of the expression is enclosed in parentheses, that portion is evaluated first. If there are nested sets of parentheses, the innermost set is evaluated first.

Example:

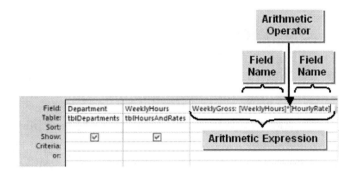

Figure 5-5: *An example of an expression.*

The Expression Builder

The Expression Builder is a tool that allows the user to select database objects and then, using the application's built-in operators and functions, build formulas and calculations that are used with queries and reports.

There are several components in the Expression Builder dialog box that allow you to create expressions.

Component	Function
The Expression box	The location where the expression is built.
The operator buttons	The location where the operators used in the expression are selected.
The left box	The location that displays the table, query, form, report object, user-defined function, and other folders.
The middle box	The location that displays the elements within the left box folder when the left box is opened.
The right box	The location that displays its related elements when the left box folder is opened and a category in the middle box is selected.

The Zoom Dialog Box

The Zoom dialog box enables you to type and view the entire expression. You can use the Zoom dialog box when an expression is too long to be displayed completely in the cell. To display the Zoom dialog box, right-click the cell and choose Zoom.

The Property Sheet Pane

The Property Sheet pane allows you to set properties for Access objects. You can specify properties such as structure, appearance, and behavior. Some of the features in the Property Sheet pane are Description, Format, Decimal Places, Input Mask, Caption, and Smart Tags.

How to Add a Calculated Field to a Query

Procedure Reference: Add a Calculated Field to a Query

To add a calculated field to a query:

1. Open the desired query and switch to Design view.
2. In the query design grid, right-click in the first available blank column and choose Build to display the Expression Builder dialog box.
3. In the Expression Builder dialog box, build the desired expression by adding the desired operators and field names and click OK.
4. If necessary, change the name of the calculated field.
5. Display the Property Sheet pane.
   - Right-click the calculated field and choose Properties.
   - Or, on the Design contextual tab, in the Show/Hide group, click Property Sheet.
6. Set the properties of the calculated field.

ACTIVITY 5-5
Creating Arithmetic Expressions

Data Files:

Arithmetic Queries.accdb

Before You Begin:

From the C:\084887Data\Querying a Database folder, open the Arithmetic Queries.accdb file.

Scenario:

You are evaluating the weekly performance of the employees and you need to calculate some performance parameters. You need to base your calculations on the data available in the company's Access database.

What You Do	How You Do It
1. **Run the qryPayRates query.**	a. **Double-click the qryPayRates query.**
	b. Observe the five fields displayed in this query, and then **switch to Design view** to view the query details.
	c. Observe that the design grid includes the tblHoursAndRates table.
2. **Use the Expression Builder to create an arithmetic expression that multiplies weekly hours by the rate of pay, and then run the query.**	a. In the design grid, in the empty column after the HourlyRate column, **right-click in the Field row and choose Build** to open the Expression Builder dialog box.
	b. In the Expression Builder operator bar, **click the equal sign (=)** to add it to the expression box.
	c. In the middle list box, **double-click WeeklyHours.**
	d. Observe that the field name is added to the expression and enclosed in brackets.
	e. In the Expression Builder operator bar, **click the multiplication sign (*)** to add it to the expression box.

f. In the middle list box, **double-click HourlyRate.**

g. **Click OK** and observe that the field name is added to the expression and is enclosed in brackets and to close the Expression Builder dialog box.

h. **Run the query.**

i. Observe that the values in the last column are the result of multiplying the WeeklyHours values by the HourlyRate values.

Department ▾	WeeklyHour ▾	HourlyRate ▾	Expr1 ▾
Technical Servi	40.0	$19.00	760
Fulfillment	40.0	$15.00	600
Finance	32.5	$12.50	406.25
Sales	35.0	$17.25	603.75
Administration	40.0	$13.95	558
Sales	40.0	$22.00	880
Administration	40.0	$14.50	580
Technical Servi	40.0	$10.00	400
Sales	40.0	$12.00	480
Sales	40.0	$15.00	600
Finance	37.5	$18.50	693.75

3. **Change the name of the calculated field to WeeklyGross.**

a. **Switch to Design view** to view the query details.

b. **Right-click the calculated field and choose Zoom.**

c. **Double-click Expr1 and type**
   WeeklyGross

WeeklyGross: [WeeklyHours]*[HourlyRate]

d. **Click OK.**

e. **Run the query.**

f. Observe that the column header for the calculated field is now named WeeklyGross.

---

4. **Open the Property Sheet pane for the WeeklyGross field and set the Format property to Currency.**

a. **Switch to Design view.**

b. **Right-click the WeeklyGross field and choose Properties.**

c. In the Property Sheet pane, **click the Format property text box.**

d. From the Format drop-down list, **select Currency and close the Property Sheet pane.**

e. **Run the query.**

f. Observe that the WeeklyGross values are now formatted as Currency values.

g. **Save and close the query and then close the database.**

TOPIC E
Perform Calculations on a Record Grouping

In the previous topic, you used a query to perform a calculation on a single record. You can group records and then perform calculations on the group. In this topic, you will create a query that selects a group of records and performs a calculation using all of the values in one of the group's fields.

Access is well suited for grouping data and performing calculations on them. One common, on-the-job use for Access is calculating payrolls. Developing a query that groups employees by department and then performs a payroll calculation on the departmental grouping will provide the results you need, and as an added benefit, you can save the query and run it as necessary.

Group By Functions

Group By functions are functions that perform calculations on a group of values. They can be used with any number of values and result in a single value. Aggregate functions are used to group records in all databases. The most commonly used aggregate functions are available for summation of values in a column, average of values in a column, count of values in a column, maximum value in a column, and minimum value in a column.

How to Perform Calculations on a Record Grouping
Procedure Reference: Perform Calculations on a Record Grouping

To perform a calculation on a group of records:

1. Open the desired query and switch to Design view.
2. In the design grid, right-click and choose Totals to add a Total row to the design grid.
3. To the design grid, add the field(s) on which you want to group records and the field(s) you wish to summarize.
4. Enter the necessary criteria to group the records you want to view.
5. If you need to enter criteria for a field on which you are not grouping records, include that field in the design grid, and from the Total drop-down list, select Where.
6. For each field, from the Total drop-down list, select Group By or the summary function.
7. Run the query.

ACTIVITY 5-6

Performing a Calculation on a Group of Records

Data Files:

Group Queries.accdb

Before You Begin:

From the C:\084887Data\Querying a Database folder, open the Group Queries.accdb file.

Scenario:

As the Finance manager of an oil company, you need to provide the average weekly hours for employees in each department and the total weekly gross payroll for each department.

What You Do	How You Do It
1. In the qryWeeklyInfo query, **add the Total row to the design grid.**	a. **Open the qryWeeklyInfo query.**
	b. **Switch to Design view** to view the query details.
	c. On the design grid, **right-click and choose Totals** to add a Total row.
2. **Remove the LastName and FirstName columns from the design grid.**	a. In the design grid, **place the mouse pointer over the LastName column heading in the design grid until it becomes a downward-pointing arrow, and click** to select the column.
	b. **Press Delete.**
	c. **Select and delete the FirstName column.**
3. **Calculate the average weekly hours for each department.**	a. **Click in the Total row for the WeeklyHours field** to display the drop-down arrow.
	b. From the drop-down list, **select Avg.**

4. In the Total row for the WeeklyGross field, **enter the summary function to calculate the total weekly gross payroll for each department.**

    a. **Click in the Total row for the WeeklyGross field** to display the drop-down arrow.

    b. From the drop-down list, **select Sum.**

    c. **Run the query.**

    d. Observe the total weekly payroll details per department.

5. **Modify the format of the WeeklyHours field to display the average weekly hours for each department with one decimal place.**

    a. **Switch to Design view.**

    b. In the WeeklyHours field, **right-click and choose Properties** to display the Property Sheet pane.

    c. In the Property Sheet pane, **click the Format property.**

    d. From the Format drop-down list, **select Fixed.**

    e. **Click the Decimal Places property,** and from the drop-down list, **select 1.**

    f. **Close the Property Sheet pane.**

    g. **Run the query.**

    h. Observe the average weekly hours being displayed.

    i. **Save and close the query and then close the database.**

Lesson 5 Follow-up

In this lesson, you created queries and filtered data using them. You also examined the various methods of creating a query. Your proficiency with queries will greatly increase your efficiency in working with databases.

1. **What are the operators that you will use when you have more than one criterion to be included in a query?**

2. **Determine the best suited method for creating a query for retrieving information from your database.**

6 | Designing Forms

Lesson Time: 35 minutes

Lesson Objectives:

In this lesson, you will design forms.

You will:

- View data using an Access form.
- Create a form.
- Modify the design of a form.

Introduction

You used queries in order to manipulate information in a database. You may now want to perform the same function using a customized user interface. In this lesson, you will design forms to enter, edit, or display data from a table.

When opening a table in Datasheet view, the entire table, including all of the records and every field in each record, is displayed. In large tables with thousands of records, this can be overwhelming. Searching for individual records or fields can be time consuming, and the chance of making an error by misreading a value is increased. Creating a customized Access form that allows you to view and edit one record at a time will expedite the process and reduce errors.

TOPIC A
View Data Using an Access Form

You used queries in order to retrieve data from a table. Now, you may want to control the way the data from a table or query is presented to users who are adding or editing data. In this topic, you will use various form views to present data in a customized format.

After designing tables and populating them with initial data, you or other users may need to enter new records, edit existing data, display the data in a certain format, or restrict access to certain fields in the table. You can do all this and more using forms.

Form Views

Access allows database users to view forms in different ways. This involves viewing a form during design, runtime, or a combination of both. The following table describes the different views.

View	Description
Design	A static view that helps you design a form. It consists of the Header, Detail, and Footer sections. A wide variety of controls, such as graphic images, can be added only in Design view.
Form	A dynamic view that allows you to view data from a table or query on which the form is based. You can use this view to add records, edit records, or navigate through a table. You will not be able to implement any changes to the design of the form in this view.
Layout	An interactive and dynamic view that you can use to create a form. You will be able to view the data bound to a control as in Form view. You can also make changes to the properties of the control, such as resizing and rearranging the control, as in Design view.

Form Sections

The *Design view* of a form consists of three general sections: the Header section at the top displays information such as the form title, the Detail section in the middle displays the table records, and the Footer section at the bottom of the form displays additional information such as the current date and page number.

Form Contextual Tabs

Depending on the form view that you select, Microsoft Access 2007 enables a context-sensitive tab that can be used to perform specific operations related to that view. These tabs are described in the following table.

Contextual Tab	Description
Format	Enabled when you open a form in Layout view. The Format contextual tab contains options that help you manage the appearance of a form.
Design	Enabled when you open a form in Design view. The Design contextual tab has a collection of tools that help you add controls such as text boxes, labels, buttons, and combo boxes to a form.
Arrange	Enabled when you open a form either in Design or Layout view. This contextual tab has a collection of tools that help you control the position, properties, and alignment of controls on the form.

The Record Navigation Bar

The Record Navigation bar in Layout and Form views helps you navigate through the recordset. You can navigate to the previous, next, first, or last record in a recordset by using the controls on the Record Navigation bar. You can also quickly jump to an empty version of the form in order to add a new record.

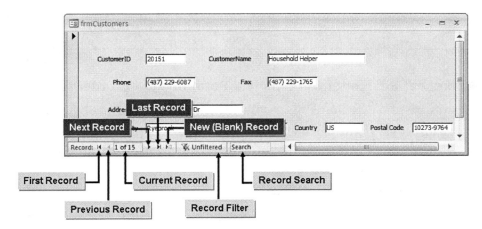

Figure 6-1: The Record Navigation bar helps you navigate through records.

How to View Data Using an Access Form

Procedure Reference: View and Add Records Using a Form

To view and add records using a form:

1. Open a form in Form view.

    *   In the Navigation Pane, right-click the desired form and choose Open.

    *   Or, in the Navigation Pane, double-click the desired form.

 Upon opening a database, if you do not find a list of forms, you will have to select the All Access Objects option from the Navigation Pane drop-down list. Selecting this option will list a set of forms, if any exist, for the current database.

2. Navigate through the records using the Record Navigation bar.

    *   Click the Next Record and Previous Record buttons to display the succeeding and preceding records in the table.

    *   Click the Last Record and First Record buttons to display the last and first records of the table.

    *   In the Current Record text box, delete the current entry, type a record number, and press Enter to display the corresponding record.

3. Add records to a table using the form.

    a. On the Record Navigation bar, click the New (Blank) Record button.

    b. In the empty form that is displayed, enter the appropriate data for the new record.

 You can open a table to verify the addition of new records that you have added using forms. This is typically not necessary, but might be advisable the first time you use a particular form.

Procedure Reference: Search for Records in a Form Based on Criteria

To search for records based on criteria:

1. Open a form and, on the Home tab, click the Find button.
2. Type the text that needs to be searched for and, if desired, set the Look In, Match Values, and other optional values in the dialog box.
3. Click Find Next to retrieve the first record that matches the search criteria.
4. If necessary, click the Find Next button to retrieve more records that match the search criteria.

Navigation in an Access Form

To move through the fields of a record displayed in a form, you can use the mouse, keys, or keystroke combinations. Different navigation methods are described in the table.

Keystroke	Used to Move To
Tab, Enter, Right Arrow, Down Arrow	The next field in a form. If you are in the last field of a record, pressing any of these keys will transfer control to the first field of the next record.
Shift+Tab, Left Arrow, Up Arrow	The previous field in a form. If you are in the first field in a form, pressing any of these keys will transfer control to the last field of the previous record.
Page Up	The same field in the previous record.
Page Down	The same field in the next record.
Home	The first field of the record you are currently in.
End	The last field of the record you are currently in.
Ctrl+Home	The first field in the first record of the table that you are currently working on.
Ctrl+End	The last field in the last record of the table that you are working in.

ACTIVITY 6-1
Using a Form to Navigate and Add Records

Data Files:

Use Forms.accdb

Setup:

From the C:\084887Data\Designing Forms folder, open the Use Forms.accdb file.

Scenario:

You have never used the Customers form before, and you have been asked to use it to add a new New York customer record to the Customers table. Therefore, you have decided to navigate through the form to familiarize yourself with it, and then search for the customers from New York to make sure the new one isn't already included. Then, you will use the form to add the new record.

What You Do	How You Do It
1. Navigate through a recordset.	a. **Open the frmCustomers form.**
	b. On the Record Navigation bar, **click the Next Record button** ▶ **two times** to view the third record of the table.
	c. On the Record Navigation bar, **click the Previous Record button** ◀ to view the second record of the table.
	d. On the Record Navigation bar, **click the Last Record button** ▶| to view the last record of the table.
	e. On the Record Navigation bar, **click the First Record button** |◀ to view the first record of the table.
	f. On the Record Navigation bar, in the Current Record text box, **place the insertion point before the text and press Delete.**
	g. **Type *4* and press Enter** to view the fourth record of the table.
	h. **Close the frmCustomers form.**

2.	**Observe the form contextual tabs.**	a.	Observe the four tabs on the Ribbon.
		b.	In the Navigation Pane, in the Forms section, **right-click frmCustomers and choose Layout View.**
		c.	Observe that the form is displayed in the Layout view and the two contextual tabs Format and Arrange are displayed.
		d.	In the Navigation Pane, in the Forms section, **right-click frmCustomers and choose Design View.**
		e.	Observe that the form opens in Design view and the Design and Arrange contextual tabs are displayed.
3.	**Find records of clients who have their headquarters in the State of New York.**	a.	**Switch to Form view.**
		b.	In the frmCustomers form, in the Region text box, **double-click the text "NY."**
		c.	On the Home tab, in the Find group, **click the Find button.**
		d.	In the Find And Replace dialog box, in the Find What text box, observe that the search criterion has been entered.
		e.	**Click Find Next.**
		f.	**Close the Find And Replace dialog box.**
		g.	Observe that the next record that matches the search criteria for clients with headquarters in the State of New York is displayed.
4.	**Use this form to add a new record to the tblCustomers table.**	a.	On the Record Navigation bar, **click the New (Blank) Record button.**
		b.	In the frmCustomers form, **click in the CustomerID text box.**
		c.	**Type *20152* and press Enter** to enter the customer ID number.

d. Similarly, enter the information in the following fields.

- CustomerName: A2Z Cleaners
- Phone: 4235554567
- Fax: 4235554568
- Address: 12 Sunshine Dr
- City: Rochester
- Region: NY
- Country: US
- Postal Code: 14603-1456

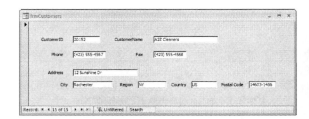

e. Close the frmCustomers form.

---

5. Observe data in tables that has been entered using forms.

a. Open the tblCustomers table.

b. Observe that the record for A2Z Cleaners has been entered.

c. Close the tblCustomers table.

d. Close the database.

TOPIC B
Create a Form

In the previous topic, you viewed the data in tables using existing forms. Now, you would like to create new forms that can be used to efficiently enter and edit data in tables. In this topic, you will create a form using various form design tools available in Access 2007.

If you are working with a reasonably large database, you may need to enter a large number of records. It may be tedious to frequently open tables and enter records. However, by using forms, you can streamline the data entry process and increase productivity.

Form Creation Tools

Access offers a host of form creation tools that can be used interchangeably, depending on the needs of the user. The following table describes the form creation tools.

Form Creation Tool	Description
Form	Creates a form that uses all the fields in a table. The form will be displayed in Layout view.
Form Design	Helps you create a form in Design view.
Split Form	Lets you view the form in Form view and Datasheet view simultaneously. Form view can be used to edit a record, while the Datasheet view can be used to navigate to a record.
Multiple Items	Lets you view multiple records from the table in the form of a spreadsheet.
PivotChart	Helps you create a form in PivotChart view. This aids in three-dimensional analysis of data.
Blank Form	Aids you in creating a blank form. You can use a blank form to build a form from scratch by adding and positioning controls according to your choice.
Form Wizard	A tool that takes you through the process of creating a form, using multiple steps. The steps help you to end up with an effective and attractive design by allowing you to specify the layout and the background themes for the form.

Form Layouts

Access provides you with four types of form layouts: Columnar, Tabular, Datasheet, and Justified. Depending on your choice on how you want to arrange data, you can choose one of these four available layouts.

How to Create a Form

Procedure Reference: Create Forms Using Various Form Creation Tools

To create forms using various form creation tools:

1. In the desired database, select a table from which you would like to create a form.

2. In the selected table, generate a form using the options in the Forms group on the Create tab.

   - Click Form to generate a simple form.
   - Click Split Form to generate a form that displays the datasheet and the form.
   - Click Multiple Items to generate a form that displays all the records in the table.
   - Click Blank Form to generate a blank form that can be customized.
   - Click Form Design to create a blank form in Design view that can be customized.
   - Click More Forms and select Datasheet to display the forms in Datasheet view.

3. Save the form.

Procedure Reference: Create a Form with the Form Wizard

To create a form with the Form Wizard:

1. On the Create tab, in the Forms group, click More Forms, and select Form Wizard.

2. From the Tables/Queries drop-down list, select the first data source for the form.

3. Add the fields you want in the form to the Selected Fields list box.

4. If necessary, add any additional data sources and fields and click Next.

5. Choose the form layout and click Next.

6. Choose the form style and click Next.

7. If necessary, provide a title for the form, select if you want to open the form or modify the form's design, and click Finish.

ACTIVITY 6-2

Creating Forms Using Form Tools

Data Files:

Forms.accdb

Setup:

From the C:\084887Data\Designing Forms folder, open the Forms.accdb file.

Scenario:

You are in charge of maintaining the employee database of your company. You realize that updating the database tables directly might be quite time consuming. To facilitate the process, you decide to simplify the task of data entry and editing by creating user-friendly interfaces for various groups of users.

What You Do	How You Do It
1. **Create a form using the Form tool.**	a. In the Navigation Pane, in the Tables section, **verify that the tblComputers table is selected.**
	b. On the Create tab, in the Forms group, **click Form.**
	c. Observe that a form has been created based on the tblComputers table.
	d. On the Quick Access toolbar, **click Save.**
	e. In the Form Name text box, **type *frmComputersFormTool* and click OK.**
	f. **Close the frmComputersFormTool form.**
2. **Create a form using the Split Form tool.**	a. On the Create tab, in the Forms group, **click Split Form.**
	b. Observe that a split form with a Layout view on top and a Datasheet view at the bottom has been created based on the tblComputers table.
	c. **Save the form as *frmComputersSplitForm*.**
	d. **Close the frmComputersSplitForm form.**

3. Create a form using the Multiple Items Form tool.	a. On the Create tab, in the Forms group, **click Multiple Items.**
	b. Observe that a form that resembles a datasheet has been created.
	c. **Save the form as *frmComputersMultipleItems*.**
	d. **Close the frmComputersMultipleItems form.**
4. Create a form using the Blank Form tool.	a. On the Create tab, in the Forms group, **click Blank Form.**
	b. Observe that a blank form, Form1, is created and a Field List task pane with the list of tables is displayed.
	c. In the Field List task pane, **expand the tblComputers table** to view the list of fields in the table.
	d. **Double-click the AssetTag field** to include the field in the form.
	e. **Include the remaining fields of the tblComputers table in the form.**
	f. **Save the form as *frmComputersBlankForm*.**
	g. **Close the Field List task pane.**
	h. **Close the frmComputersBlankForm form.**
	i. In the Navigation Pane, in the Forms section, **double-click frmComputersBlankForm** to view the form at runtime.
	j. Observe the employee details displayed in the fields in the form.
	k. **Close the frmComputersBlankForm form.**

5. **Create a form using the Form Design tool.**

   a. In the Navigation Pane, in the Tables section, **select the tblComputers table.**

   b. On the Create tab, in the Forms group, **click Form Design.**

   c. Observe that a blank form, Form1, is created and opened in Design view.

   d. If necessary, on the Form Design Tools Design contextual tab, in the Tools group, **click Add Existing Fields.**

   e. In the Field List task pane, observe the list of fields in the tblComputers table.

   f. **Double-click the AssetTag field to** include it in the form.

   g. **Include the remaining fields of the tblComputers table in the form.**

   h. **Save the form as** *frmComputersFormDesign.*

   i. **Close the Field List task pane.**

   j. **Close the frmComputersFormDesign form.**

   k. **Close the database.**

ACTIVITY 6-3
Creating a Form with the Form Wizard

Data Files:

Form Wizard.accdb

Setup:

From the C:\084887Data\Designing Forms folder, open the Form Wizard.accdb file.

Scenario:

You have a database in which you maintain information about employees and the computer systems assigned to them. Recently, there has been a major shuffling of employees and their computers. To facilitate the updating process for the computers data, you have been asked to quickly design an interface. You also need to create an appropriate layout and style for the form.

What You Do	How You Do It
1. **Add the required fields from the tblComputers table to the form.**	a. On the Create tab, in the Forms group, **Click More Forms and select Form Wizard.**
	b. In the Form Wizard dialog box, in the Tables/Queries section, observe that the tblComputers table has been selected.
	c. **Click the Add All button** `>>` **and click Next** to add all the fields of the table in the Available Fields list box to the Selected Fields list box and proceed to the next screen.
2. **Select a layout and style for the form.**	a. **Select Tabular and click Next.**
	b. In the list box, **select Access 2007 and click Next.**

3.   Create the form.

a.   In the What Title Do You Want For Your Form text box, **double-click tblComputers and type** *frmComputersFormWizard*

b.   Under Do You Want To Open The Form Or Modify The Form's Design, **verify that Open The Form To View Or Enter Information is selected and click Finish.**

c.   Observe the form that has been created using the wizard.

d.   **Close the frmComputersFormWizard form.**

e.   **Close the database.**

TOPIC C
Modify the Design of a Form

In the previous topic, you learned how to create forms using the various form creation tools. After creating a form, you may need to customize the form design to suit your needs. In this topic, you will examine the methods for modifying the design of a form.

In certain instances, in order to simplify the task of data entry, you might want to restructure the logical flow of information in a form and not follow the same sequence as is present in the table on which the form is based. In those cases, it becomes absolutely essential to modify the design of the form.

The Tab Order

The logical flow of information in a form is indicated by the use of the Tab key. This flow is better known as the tab order. Selecting a control in a form and then pressing the Tab key will move the focus to the next field that is in line with the flow of information in the form.

Controls

Definition:

A *control* is an object placed on user interfaces that allows the user to interact with the application. Controls are used to display data, obtain user input, perform an action, or enhance the user interface. Controls are commonly used in forms and reports. Controls can be selected, sized, aligned, and moved. They are generally labeled with context-significant names so that users can identify their purpose.

Example:

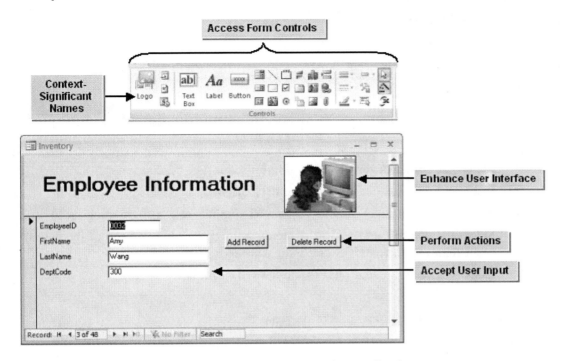

Figure 6-2: A control allows the user to interact with the application.

Types of Controls

The controls placed on a form can be broadly classified into three types depending on the type of data they are associated with. These types are described in the following table.

Control Type	Description
Bound control	Associated with data from a field in a table or query. You can use bound controls to retrieve and display data from a table.
Unbound control	A static control that is not associated with any data in any table or query.
Calculated control	A control that displays data obtained by evaluating an arithmetic expression.

How to Modify the Design of a Form

Procedure Reference: Modify a Form

To modify a form:

1. Open a form in Design view.

2. Select the controls you need to work with.

3. If necessary, move the controls.

    ●   Move just the text box or label and not its associated component.

        a. Select the control and move the mouse pointer on top of the square near the upper-left corner of the control until you see a four-headed arrow.

        b. Click and drag the control(s) to the desired position.

    ●   Move the text box or label (and its associated component), or a grouping of controls.

        a. Select the controls and move the mouse pointer anywhere on top of the control other than the upper-left corner until you see a four-headed arrow.

        b. Click and drag the control(s) to the desired position.

4. If necessary, resize the controls.

    ●   Drag a sizing handle to increase or decrease the size.

    ●   Or, on the Arrange contextual tab, in the Size group, click the Size To Fit button.

 You can access the same options available on the Arrange contextual tab by right-clicking a selected control and choosing Size→To Fit.

5. Align the controls.

    a. Select the controls you want to align.

    b. Right-click the selected controls, choose Align, and select the option to set the appropriate position.

    c. Select the controls and resize them in order to adjust their spacing.

6. If necessary, adjust the tab order of the form fields.

    a. On the Arrange contextual tab, in the Control Layout group, click Tab Order.

    b. In the Tab Order dialog box, set the tab order.

        ●   Click Auto Order and then click OK.

        ●   In the Custom Order box, select a field, or multiple fields, and drag them to the desired tab order and click OK.

7. If desired, on the Design contextual tab, apply formatting to text boxes or labels and click Title to apply a title.

8. If necessary, resize the form window to change the size of the form.

ACTIVITY 6-4
Modifying a Form

Data Files:

FormTabOrder.accdb

Setup:

From the C:\084887Data\Designing Forms folder, open the Form Tab Order.accdb file.

Scenario:

As part of a new venture in your organization to improve user interfaces in applications, you have been asked to modify the appearance of an existing form.

What You Do	How You Do It
1. **Arrange the controls on the form.**	a. In the Navigation Pane, **right-click frmGSCCustomers and choose Design View.**
	b. If necessary, **close the Field List pane.**
	c. **Click to the left of the CustomerName label and text box controls to select them, and then drag the fields to the right of the CustomerID control.**
	d. **Click to the left of the Address field and drag until the end of the Fax control to select all the fields below CustomerID.**
	e. **Press the Down arrow key seven times** so that you have room to arrange the Phone and Fax controls in the space below the CustomerID and CustomerName controls.

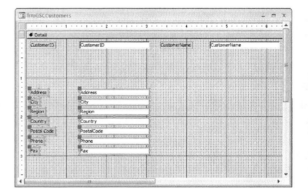

	f. **Click the empty form area** to deselect the fields.
	g. **Select and drag the Phone label and text box to place it below the CustomerID control.**
	h. **Click the empty form area** to deselect the fields.
	i. **Select and drag the Fax label and text box to place it below the CustomerName control.**

j. **Drag the Address, City, Region, Country, and Postal Code field controls** to place them below the Phone field control.

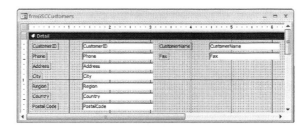

k. **Click the empty form area** to deselect the fields.

l. **Save the form.**

2. **Switch to Form view** to check the tab order.

a. **Switch to Form view.**

b. **Press Tab eight times** to move from the first field in the form to the last.

c. Observe that the Phone field logically follows the CustomerName field in the form's new layout, but the tab order is based on the original layout.

3. **Open the form in Design view** to correct the tab order.

a. **Switch to Design view.**

b. On the Arrange contextual tab, in the Control Layout group, **click Tab Order.**

c. In the Tab Order dialog box, **click Auto Order and then click OK.**

4. **Return to Form view and check the tab order.**

   a. **Switch to Form view.**

   b. **Press Tab eight times** to move through the fields.

   c. Observe that the tab order has been corrected to better suit the form's new layout.

   d. **Save and close the form.**

   e. **Close the database.**

Lesson 6 Follow-up

In this lesson, you learned the techniques of creating forms using various form design tools. By grouping and aligning form controls and making other aesthetic improvements, you will be able to design custom forms that will help users feel more comfortable while entering data.

1. **How will you arrive at the choice of the correct tool for designing your forms?**

2. **Do you expect to make more aesthetic improvements to your forms or more improvements to enhance data entry efficiency? Or both?**

7 | Generating Reports

Lesson Time: 45 minutes

Lesson Objectives:

In this lesson, you will generate reports.

You will:

- View an Access report.
- Create a report.
- Add a custom calculated field to a report.
- Format the controls in a report.
- Apply an AutoFormat style to a report.
- Prepare a report for print.

Introduction

You created forms in order to view and manipulate the data in individual records. However, when you need to make decisions based on this data, you may want to generate a report summarizing the data. In this lesson, you will use the Access report development and design tools in order to create reports.

Assume that the total sales of your company have dropped during the current fiscal year. Information on every product sold is currently held in a large database in your company. You can use the reporting feature of the database to arrive at a better understanding of the total sales for each product, region, and salesperson. You can take corrective measures based on these reports.

TOPIC A
View an Access Report

In the previous lesson, you designed forms in order to view and edit data through a friendly interface. However, when it comes to viewing and analyzing large amounts of data, reports are a better option than forms. In this topic, you will view an Access report to give you an understanding of what it is all about before designing your own.

In every organization, managers make decisions based on the performance reports that they receive from all quarters. Viewing all the data in all the records in a table to make a decision can result in data overload and be a very inefficient approach. Reports group and summarize data and facilitate the decision-making process.

Report Views

To edit and modify reports, Access 2007 provides four views. Your choice of which to use will depend on the task you need to perform with your reports.

View	Description
Design	You will be able to add, modify, or delete controls such as labels and images with much ease in Design view. However, you will not be able to view the underlying data associated with each control.
Report	You will be able to view data from a table or query on which the report is based. You will not be able to implement any changes to the design or the underlying data for each control in this view.
Layout	You will be able to view the data bound to a control and make changes to the properties of the controls such as resizing and rearranging the controls as in a Design view.
Print Preview	You will be able to check how your report may look when printed on paper. You can use the various options on the Print Preview tab to set the report page layout before you go ahead and print the report.

Report Sections

The Design view of a report consists of a header and footer band for the report, page, and group sections. While information that needs to appear on every page of a printed report is entered in the page header and footer, information that needs to appear for each group of data is entered in the group header and footer. Information that only needs to appear once, at the top and bottom of the report, is entered in the report header and footer, respectively. The Detail section in the middle displays the table records.

Report Contextual Tabs

Depending on the task that you need to perform using your reports, one or many context-sensitive tabs get enabled.

Contextual Tab	Description
Format	Enabled when you open a report in the Layout view and has options that help you manage the appearance of a report.
Arrange	Enabled when a report is opened in either the Design or Layout view. This tab has a collection of tools that help you control the position, properties, and alignment of controls on the report.
Page Setup	Enabled in both the Design and Layout views. The options on this tab help you set the paper margins and perform other operations such as choosing the paper size.
Design	Enabled when you open a report in Design view. This tab has a collection of tools that help you add controls such as text boxes, labels, buttons, and combo boxes to a report. Formatting options are also available as part of this tab.
Print Preview	Enabled when you choose the Print Preview view, and contains options that help set the report page layout.

How to View an Access Report

Procedure Reference: View an Access Report in Different Views

To view an Access report in different views:

1. If necessary, click the Navigation Pane drop-down arrow and select Reports to display the list of reports in the database.

2. Open the desired report.

    ● In the Navigation Pane, double-click the desired report.

    ● Or, in the Navigation Pane, right-click the desired report and choose Open.

3. View the report in different views.

    ● View the report in Report view.

    ■ Right-click the report document tab and choose Report View.

    ■ On the Microsoft Office status bar, click the Report View button.

    ■ Or, on the Home tab, click the View drop-down arrow and select Report View.

    ● View the report in Design view.

    ■ Right-click the report document tab and choose Design View.

    ■ On the Microsoft Office status bar, click the Design View button.

    ■ Or, on the Home tab, click the View drop-down arrow and select Design View.

    ● View the report in Layout view.

    ■ Right-click the report document tab and choose Layout View.

    ■ On the Microsoft Office status bar, click the Layout View button.

    ■ Or, on the Home tab, click the View drop-down arrow and select Layout View.

    ● View the print preview of the report.

    ■ Right-click the report document tab and choose Print Preview.

    ■ Or, on the Microsoft Office status bar, click the Print Preview button.

Procedure Reference: Navigate Through an Access Report in Print Preview Mode

To navigate through an Access report in Print Preview mode:

1. If necessary, click the Navigation Pane drop-down arrow and select Reports to display the list of reports in the database.

2. Display the desired report in Print Preview mode.

3. Navigate through the report using the Navigation Bar.

ACTIVITY 7-1

Viewing an Access Report

Data Files:

Inventory.accdb

Before You Begin:

From the C:\084887Data\Generating Reports folder, open the Inventory.accdb file.

Scenario:

As the Public Relations Executive of your company, you need to provide your client with details about your company. You want to create reports based on the information in your company's databases. As you have not worked with reports earlier, you first want to explore an Access report before setting off to create one.

What You Do	How You Do It
1. Display the report contextual tabs.	a. **Click the Navigation Pane drop-down arrow and select Reports** to display the list of reports in the database.
	b. In the Navigation Pane, **right-click rptFinalReport and choose Layout View** to open the report in Layout view.
	c. Observe that the Format, Arrange, and Page Setup contextual tabs are displayed on the Ribbon.

2. View the report in different views.

a. On the Microsoft Office status bar, **click the Design View button.** ▨

b. Observe the various sections of the report such as the header and the footer.

c. On the Design contextual tab, in the Views group, **click the View drop-down arrow and select Report View.**

d. Observe that the report is displayed in Report view.

e. **Right-click the report document tab and choose Print Preview.**

f. Observe that the report is displayed in Print Preview mode and the Print Preview tab is displayed on the Ribbon.

g. **Click anywhere on the report** to make the page fit in the document window.

3. Navigate through the report.

a. On the Navigation Bar, in the Current Page text box, **triple-click, type *3* and press Enter.**

b. On the Navigation Bar, **click the First Page button** to view the first page of the report.

c. **Click the Next Page button** ▶ to view the next page.

d. On the Print Preview tab, in the Close Preview group, **click Close Print Preview** to close the print preview of the report.

e. **Close the database.**

TOPIC B
Create a Report

In the previous topic, you viewed the data in existing reports. Now, you would like to create custom reports in order to analyze data that can be subsequently printed. In this topic, you will create a report using various report design tools available in Access 2007.

When you create a report, you may want to select only a few relevant fields from the table or, if the table contains confidential information, you may want to leave those fields out of the report. Access offers you a variety of report creation tools that help custom select the fields from the table.

Report Creation Tools

Reports can be created based on data from tables or queries. Reports can be created using one of the many report creation tools offered by Access 2007.

Tool	*Description*
Report	Creates a report that uses all the fields in a table or a query. The report will be displayed in Layout view.
Blank Report	Aids you in creating a blank report from scratch by adding and positioning controls according to your choice.
Report Design	Helps you create a report in Design view.
Report Wizard	Helps you create a report by following a step-by-step guided approach. It offers options for grouping and sorting data. It also offers design choices such as customizing layout options. Further, it helps you analyze data from one or more tables by providing you options for summarizing data using aggregate functions.

Summary Options

Access 2007 allows you to summarize data by providing aggregate functions for numeric fields in a table. Using the Summary Options dialog box, you can choose aggregate functions such as sum, average, minimum, and maximum values to be used on numeric fields in a table. There are also options to display all the records and the result returned by the aggregate function for a group of data. You can also display only the result returned by the aggregate function for a group of data.

List of Summary Options

Access 2007 provides a variety of aggregate functions such as Sum, Average, Count, Maximum, and Minimum that can be deployed on numeric fields.

How to Create a Report

Procedure Reference: Create a Blank Report

To create a blank report:

1. On the Create tab, in the Reports group, click Blank Report.
2. Save the report with the desired name.

Procedure Reference: Create a Report Based on the Data in a Table

To create a report based on the data in a table:

1. In the Navigation Pane, select the desired table.
2. On the Create tab, in the Reports group, click Report.
3. Save the report with the desired name.

Procedure Reference: Create a Report Using the Report Wizard

To create a report using the Report Wizard:

1. On the Create tab, in the Reports group, click Report Wizard.
2. In the Report Wizard, from the Tables/Queries drop-down list, select the desired table/ query and add the desired field(s) to the Selected Fields list box.
3. If necessary, from the Tables/Queries drop-down list, select another table/query and add the desired fields in the Selected Fields list box. Click Next.
4. If necessary, set the desired view options. Click Next.
5. If necessary, set the desired grouping options. Click Next.
6. If necessary, set the desired sort and summary options. Click Next.
7. Set the layout options.
    *   In the Layout section, select the desired option.
    *   In the Orientation section, select the desired option (Portrait or Landscape).
    *   Check the Adjust The Field Width So All Fields Fit On A Page check box to adjust the field width for all the fields to fit into a page.
8. Click Next.
9. On the What Style Would You Like page, in the list box, select the desired style. Click Next.
10. In the What Title Do You Want For Your Report text box, type the desired title.
11. Set the preview option.
    *   In the Do You Want To Preview The Report Or Modify The Report's Design section, select the Preview The Report option in order to view the print format of the report.
    *   In the Do You Want To Preview The Report Or Modify The Report's Design section, select the Modify The Report's Design option in order to change the design of the report.
12. Click Finish to create the report with all the specified details.

ACTIVITY 7-2

Creating a Report

Data Files:

Inventory Report.accdb

Before You Begin:

From the C:\084887Data\Generating Reports folder, open the Inventory Report.accdb file.

Scenario:

Your manager has invited you to a meeting to discuss the computer inventory of the company. To make things easier, you decide to go prepared for the meeting with important details of the allocation of computers, which is available in a table in your company's database.

What You Do	How You Do It
1. Open the tblComputers table.	a. **From the Navigation Pane drop-down list, select All Access Objects.**
	b. **Open the tblComputers table.**
	c. Observe that the tblComputers table contains data in fields such as AssetTag, ManufacturerID, DateReceived, PurchasePrice, Warranty, and EmployeeID.
2. Generate a report based on the data in the tblComputers table.	a. On the Create tab, in the Reports group, **click Report.**
	b. Observe that a report containing the data of the tblComputers table is generated.
	c. On the Quick Access toolbar, **click Save.**
	d. In the Report Name text box, **type *rptComputers***
	e. **Close the report and table.**

ACTIVITY 7-3

Creating a Report Using the Report Wizard

Before You Begin:

The Inventory Report.accdb file is open.

Scenario:

You want to create a professional-looking report that contains the purchase information of computers that were bought in your company. From the database that stores this information, you need data from multiple tables to be displayed in a specific order. Also, you want the report to display data in a particular style and layout so that your report's format matches the standard format of your company's business reports.

What You Do	How You Do It
1. **Display the Report Wizard dialog box and specify the required fields.**	a. On the Create tab, in the Reports group, **click Report Wizard.**
	b. Observe that the Report Wizard dialog box has been displayed.
	c. In the Report Wizard, from the Tables/Queries drop-down list, **select Table: tblDepartments.**
	d. **Add the DeptCode field to the Selected Fields list box.**
	e. From the Tables/Queries drop-down list, **select Table: tblComputers.**
	f. **Add the AssetTag field to the Selected Fields list box.**
	g. **Add the ManufacturerID, DateReceived, and PurchasePrice fields to the Selected Fields list box.**
	h. **Click Next** to move to the next page.
	i. **Click Next** to accept the default view options.
	j. **Click Next** to skip the grouping options.

2. Set the summary option.

  a. **Click Summary Options.**

  b. In the Summary Options dialog box, in the Field section, **verify that PurchasePrice is displayed.**

  c. **Check the Sum check box.**

  d. In the Show section, **verify that the Detail And Summary option is selected and click OK** to close the Summary Options dialog box.

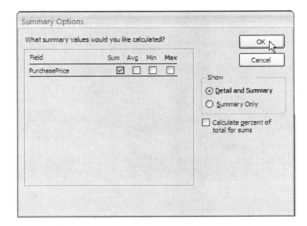

  e. In the Report Wizard dialog box, **click Next.**

3. Set the layout and style for the report.

  a. In the Layout section, **select the Block option.**

  b. In the Orientation section, **verify that the Portrait option is selected.**

  c. **Verify that the Adjust The Field Width So All Fields Fit On A Page check box is checked and click Next** to move to the next page.

  d. On the What Style Would You Like page, in the list box, **select Concourse and click Next.**

4. Specify the title for the report.

  a. In the What Title Do You Want For Your Report text box, **double-click and type *rptPurchaseInfo***

b. In the Do You Want To Preview The Report Or Modify The Report's Design section, **verify that the Preview The Report option is selected and click Finish.**

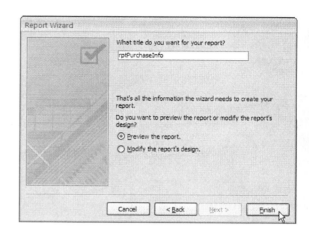

c. Observe that a report has been created with all the specified details.

d. **Close the report and the database.**

TOPIC C
Add a Custom Calculated Field to a Report

In the previous topic, you created reports using the various report creation tools. However, there might be instances where you need to calculate values during report execution and display the calculated values as an additional field in the report. In this topic, you will add a field to a report that will display the result of an arithmetic calculation.

You may need to perform calculations on table and query data. One such instance would be during the holiday season, when commercial establishments come up with various promotional offers and sell products at discounted prices. A new price list will need to be generated based on the original prices. Instead of doing it manually, you can accomplish this by adding a simple calculated field, which returns the final product price after the discount in your report.

How to Add a Custom Calculated Field to a Report
Procedure Reference: Add a Custom Calculated Field to a Report

To add a custom calculated field to a report:

1. Display the desired report in Design view.
2. On the Design contextual tab, in the Controls group, click the Text Box button.
3. In the report document window, click in the section where you want to add the calculated control.
4. Display the Property Sheet pane, and on the Data or All tab, click the Control Source property.
5. Click the Build button to display the Expression Builder dialog box.
6. In the Expression Builder dialog box, build the desired expression by adding the desired operators and field names and click OK to close the Expression Builder dialog box.
7. If necessary, close the Property Sheet pane.
8. In the report document window, remove the default label control or type the desired name for the calculated field.
9. Save the report.

ACTIVITY 7-4
Adding a Custom Calculated Field to a Report

Data Files:

Inventory Calc.accdb

Before You Begin:

From the C:\084887Data\Generating Reports folder, open the Inventory Calc.accdb file.

Scenario:

As the Accounts Manager of your company, you have created a report based on the purchase information of computers. You would like to amortize the cost of the computers over three years and include the result in the report.

What You Do	How You Do It
1. Insert a text box control into the report.	a. Open the **rptDepartmentalInventory report in Design view.**
	b. On the Design contextual tab, in the Controls group, **click the Text Box button.** abl
	c. On the rptDepartmentalInventory report tab, in the Detail section, **click to the right of the PurchasePrice control** to add a new control.
2. Display the Expression Builder dialog box.	a. In the Tools group, **click Property Sheet** to display the Property Sheet pane.
	b. In the Property Sheet pane, **verify that the All tab is selected.**
	c. On the All tab, **click the Control Source property.**
	d. **Click the Build button** [...], to display the Expression Builder dialog box.

3. **Add a custom calculation to the selected control.**

a. On the Expression Builder operator bar, **click the equal sign (=)** to add it to the expression box.

b. In the middle list box, **scroll down and double-click PurchasePrice** to add it to the expression box.

c. On the Expression Builder operator bar, **click the division sign (/)** to add it to the expression box.

d. **Type** *3*.

e. **Verify that the required expression = [PurchasePrice] / 3 is displayed in the expression box and click OK.**

`= [PurchasePrice] / 3 |`   OK   Cancel   Undo

4. Insert a label for the calculated field.

a. **Close the Property Sheet pane.**

b. On the rptDepartmentalInventory report tab, in the Detail section, **click the default label control that was created with the text box control.**

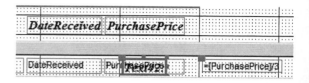

c. **Press Delete** to delete the control.

d. In the Controls group, **click the Label (Form Control) button.**

e. In the report document window, in the LastName Header section, to the right of the PurchasePrice label, **click and drag** to create a label control.

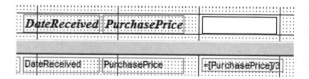

f. In the label control, **type *Amortized***

g. **Click the Office button and choose Save As.**

h. In the Save As dialog box, **type *rptMyInventory* and click OK.**

i. On the Microsoft Office status bar, **click the Report View button** to display the report in Report view.

j. Observe that the report displays the Amortized field with the calculated values.

k. **Close the table.**

TOPIC D
Format the Controls in a Report

You may have used the Report Wizard to show summary information in a report. However, at times, you might be required to change the way data is displayed in a control based on user requirements. In this topic, you will format the controls in a report in order to customize the way data is displayed.

Assume that you are preparing a financial report for your organization. The Report Wizard can help you generate a comprehensive state-of-the-art report. However, you may want to tweak the way data is displayed in certain sections of the report, such as the annual turnover and the profit and loss section, to catch the user's attention. This is easily accomplished by formatting controls to display data as desired.

Control Properties

You can access the property of a control by using the Property Sheet pane. The Property Sheet pane categorizes the information to be formatted into four different tabs: Format, Data, Event, and Other. The Format tab allows you to define the format in which data has to be displayed. The *Control Source Property* allows you to define or edit the data source of a control in a report.

How to Format the Controls in a Report
Procedure Reference: Format a Control in a Report

To format a control in a report:

1. Display the desired report in Design view.
2. In the report document window, select the desired control.
3. Display the Property Sheet pane and select the Format tab.
4. On the Format tab, click the Format property, and from the Format drop-down list, select the desired option. The most common options are Currency, Fixed, Euro, and Scientific.
5. Set other property settings as desired.
6. Save the report.

ACTIVITY 7-5
Formatting the Controls in a Report

Before You Begin:
The Inventory Calc.accdb is open, and the rptMyInventory report is displayed in Report view.

Scenario:
You have created a business report using Access. While reviewing the report, you think the data contained in a particular field can be comprehended more easily if it is formatted appropriately. Also, you want to change the format of the date, thereby making your report look more professional.

What You Do	How You Do It
1. **Change the format of the control containing the amortization expression to currency.**	a. In the report, observe that the values under the Amortized field are in general number format, and in some cases have long decimals.
	b. **Switch to Design view.**
	c. On the rptMyInventory report tab, in the Detail section, **select the control containing the =[PurchasePrice]/3 expression.**
	d. On the Design contextual tab, in the Tools group, **click Property Sheet.**
	e. In the Property Sheet pane, **select the Format tab.**
	f. From the Format drop-down list, **select Currency.**
	g. **Close the Property Sheet pane.**
	h. **Switch to Report view.**

i. In the report, observe that the values under the Amortized field are in the currency format.

Amortized

$433.33

Amortized

$400.00

---

2. **Change the format of the control displaying the date to short date.**

a. In the report, observe that the date is displayed in long form.

b. **Switch to Design view.**

c. In the report document window, in the Report Header section, **right-click the control containing the =Now() function and choose Properties** to display the Property Sheet pane.

d. On the Format tab, from the Format drop-down list, **select Short Date.**

e. **Close the Property Sheet pane.**

f. **Switch to Report view.**

g. In the report, observe that the date is displayed in short form.

h. **Save and close the report.**

i. **Close the database.**

TOPIC E
Apply an AutoFormat Style to a Report

You designed reports using a variety of built-in style options in the Report Wizard. At times, you might be required to change the design style for an existing report without re-creating the entire report. In this topic, you will apply an AutoFormat style to a report.

Imagine that you have created a report that is to be used by several different departments in the organization. You now want to create the same report using a different style for a marketing presentation. Creating the report again from scratch could consume a lot of time. The AutoFormat feature of Access allows you to change the appearance of a report with less effort and time.

AutoFormat

The AutoFormat feature for reports allows you to apply a predefined design format to an existing report. You can choose a new format from the AutoFormat gallery to be applied to the current report. By selecting the AutoFormat Wizard in the AutoFormat gallery, you can display the AutoFormat dialog box. You can also customize the design formats.

How to Apply an AutoFormat Style to a Report

Procedure Reference: Apply an AutoFormat Style to a Report in Layout View

To apply an AutoFormat style to a report in Layout view:

1. Display the desired report in Layout view.
2. On the Ribbon, on the Format contextual tab, in the AutoFormat group, click AutoFormat, and from the AutoFormat gallery, select the desired style to apply to the report.
3. Save the report.

Procedure Reference: Apply an AutoFormat Style to a Report in Design View

To apply an AutoFormat style to a report in Design view:

1. Display the desired report in Design view.
2. On the Ribbon, on the Arrange contextual tab, in the AutoFormat group, click AutoFormat, and from the AutoFormat gallery, select the desired style to apply to the report.
3. Save the report.

ACTIVITY 7-6

Applying an AutoFormat Style to a Report

Data Files:

Inventory Format.accdb

Before You Begin:

From the C:\084887Data\Generating Reports folder, open the Inventory Format.accdb file.

Scenario:

As the Accounts Manager of your company, you have created a report based on the purchase information of computers that were bought during the last month. You are not pleased with the format of the report. You could attempt to adjust a number of properties and controls, but you realize that you do not have enough time to try that out. So, you decide to use the quickest method in order to change the format of the report.

What You Do	How You Do It
1. Display the rptDepartments report in Layout view.	a. Open the rptDepartments report.
	b. Switch to Layout view.

2. Apply an AutoFormat style to the report.

a. On the Ribbon, **verify that the Format contextual tab is selected.**

b. In the AutoFormat group, **click AutoFormat,** and in the AutoFormat gallery, in the fourth row, in the second column, **select the Opulent style.**

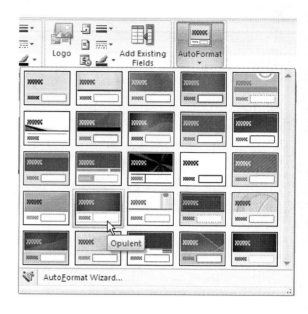

c. Observe that the selected style has been applied to the report.

d. **Save the report as** *rptMyDepartments* **and close it**.

e. **Close the database.**

TOPIC F
Prepare a Report for Print

In the previous topic, you generated a report consisting of all the fields from a table. Reports are mostly created to be printed. There are times when a report contains so much information that the data to be displayed exceeds the size of the display area. In this topic, you will modify the margin settings to prepare a report for printing.

Though you may share electronic copies of a report, you may frequently need to print it for meetings. With printed reports or other documents, you may encounter issues such as the data overflowing the page margins or blank pages being printed. It is important that you define the page setup options before printing your report to prevent data from overflowing the page margins.

Page Setup Options

The Page Setup tab is automatically enabled in the Design and the Layout views. This tab is a collection of tools that help you set the paper size, report margins, and the direction of printing before printing the report.

Using the options on the Page Setup tab, you can customize page properties before printing your report.

Option	Allows You To
Size	Choose the size of the paper.
Portrait	Print the report along the length of the paper.
Landscape	Print the report along the breadth of the paper.
Margins	Set the margins of the paper before printing. It offers you three options to choose from: Normal, Wide, and Narrow.
Show Margins	View the margins on the console window.
Print Data Only	Print the data alone without column headers.
Columns	Divide the entire page into two or more columns.
Page Setup	Open the Page Setup dialog box.

Print Preview

The Print Preview tab provides a set of tools that help you view your report in a print layout. Using the various groups in the Print Preview tab, you can set the page layout, set the zoom size, and export the report into other formats. After previewing your report, you can print it.

Proofing Options

Access can help you prepare error-free reports by using the Proofing category of the Access Options dialog box. You can have Access automatically correct and format the contents of your database by using the Spell Check and AutoCorrect features.

How to Prepare a Report for Print

Procedure Reference: Preview a Report

To preview a report:

1. Display the desired report in Print Preview mode.
   - In the Navigation Pane, right-click the desired report and choose Print Preview.
   - Or, double-click the desired report.
2. With the Print Preview tab active, preview the report.
   - In the Zoom group, click One Page to view one page at a time.
   - In the Zoom group, click Two Pages to view two pages at a time.
   - Preview the report using the More Pages button.
      - In the Zoom group, click More Pages and select Four Pages to view four pages at a time.
      - In the Zoom group, click More Pages and select Eight Pages to view eight pages at a time.
      - In the Zoom group, click More Pages and select Twelve Pages to view 12 pages at a time.

Procedure Reference: Change the Margin Settings of a Report

To change the margin settings of a report:

1. Display the desired report in Print Preview mode.
2. With the Print Preview tab active, display the Page Setup dialog box.
   - In the Page Layout group, click Page Setup.
   - In the Page Layout group, click the Dialog Box Launcher button on the right.
   - Or, right-click anywhere in the report document window and choose Page Setup.
3. Change the margin settings of the report (Top, Bottom, Left, and Right).
4. Click OK to apply the changes.

Procedure Reference: Change the Proofing Options

To change the proofing options:

1. Click the Office button and click Access Options.
2. In the Access Options dialog box, in the left pane, select the Proofing category.
3. In the right pane, select the desired options and click OK to apply the changes.

ACTIVITY 7-7

Preparing a Report for Print

Data Files:

Inventory Print.accdb

Before You Begin:

From the C:\084887Data\Generating Reports folder, open the Inventory Print.accdb file.

Scenario:

You have created a business report and are ready to print it. As you expect a perfect output, you decide to check and alter the page settings of the report before generating a paper copy of it.

What You Do	How You Do It
1. Preview a report.	a. **Open the rptFixMargins report.**
	b. Observe that the report is displayed in Print Preview mode and the Print Preview tab is displayed on the Ribbon.
	c. In the Zoom group, **click More Pages and select Four Pages** to view four pages at a time.
	d. In the report document window, observe that the second and fourth pages of the report are blank, because of the wide margin settings.

2. **Change the margins of the report to eliminate blank pages.**

   a. In the Page Layout group, **click the Dialog Box Launcher button** on the right to display the Page Setup dialog box.

   b. In the Page Setup dialog box, **verify that the Print Options tab is selected.**

   c. On the Print Options tab, in the Margins (Inches) section, in the Left text box, **double-click and type *0.75***

   d. In the Right text box, **double-click, type *0.75* and click OK** to apply the changes.

   e. In the report document window, observe that the blank pages of the report have been removed.

   f. **Save the report as *rptMyMargins.***

   g. **Close the report and database.**

Lesson 7 Follow-up

In this lesson, you generated reports using the various report creation tools. You will now be able to produce custom reports according to your needs to help you analyze data effectively and make better decisions.

1. **In your job, would you need to create reports that retrieve data from multiple tables? What tools would you use to do this?**

2. **What uses can you think of for calculated fields in your reports?**

Follow-up

In this course, you examined the basic database concepts and accomplished various tasks using the basic features and components of Access 2007. In addition, you created and modified databases, tables, queries, forms, and reports. You have also begun to prepare for the more advanced Access courses and have completed the first step toward obtaining your Microsoft Certified Applications Specialist (MCAS) certification.

1. **How can relational databases help you manage large amounts of data?**

2. **How helpful can forms be when working with data in a database?**

3. **How do you think you can improve the appearance of forms and reports?**

What's Next?

The *Microsoft® Office Access 2007: Level 1* course introduced you to the basics of the Access application and prepared you for the Element K course, *Microsoft® Office Access 2007: Level 2.*

Lesson Labs

Due to classroom setup constraints, some labs cannot be keyed in sequence immediately following their associated lesson. Your instructor will tell you whether your labs can be practiced immediately following the lesson or whether they require separate setup from the main lesson content.

Lesson 1 Lab 1

Exploring the Various Elements of the Access Environment

Activity Time: 15 minutes

Objective:

Explore the Access interface.

Data Files:

Personnel.accdb

Scenario:

Using Access 2007, you want to create a database to store data pertaining to your company's financial transactions made during the previous financial year. To avoid possible rework later, you first want to familiarize yourself with the Access environment.

1. Launch the Microsoft Office Access 2007 application.

2. From the C:\084887Data\Exploring the Access Environment folder, **open the Personnel.accdb file.**

3. **Explore the groups and commands under each tab on the Ribbon.**

4. On the Ribbon, **select any of the core tabs** to view the various groups of commands.

5. **Open and view each of the database objects using the Navigation Pane.**

6. **Display and select a contextual tab** to view the various groups of commands.

7. **Launch a dialog box using the Dialog Box Launcher button and view the options.**

8. **Add the New button to the Quick Access toolbar.**

9. **Explore and use the Access Help feature** to find information on any desired functionality.

10. **Close the current database and exit Access.**

Lesson 2 Lab 1

Planning a Human Resources Database

Activity Time: 15 minutes

Objective:

Plan a human resources database.

Scenario:

You are responsible for designing your company's human resources database to track employees and information related to them, including personal data, department, pay rate and benefits, and parking lot assignment. Following the database design process, you need to create an appropriate design plan that includes a statement of purpose, a list of appropriate tables, and the fields in each table with primary and foreign key assignments.

---

1. Based on the assignment you have been given, **write an appropriate statement of purpose for this database.**

---

2. After looking at the available sources of data and discussing this project with the various users and stakeholders, you've decided you need to include the following fields: Name, Address, City, State, Zip, WorkPhone, DateHired, Hours, PayRate, Health, ParkName, ParkFee, and DeptName. Using this field list, **organize the fields into logical tables.**

---

3. Using the normalization guidelines, **normalize your list of tables by moving, splitting, or adding fields as necessary. Include any additional fields that will be needed to uniquely identify each record in each table and to relate the tables together.**

---

4. **Designate fields to be used as primary and foreign keys for each table.**

---

5. **Identify the relationships between these tables.**

Lesson 3 Lab 1

Building a Customer Database

Activity Time: 10 minutes

Objective:

Build a customer database.

Before You Begin:

Launch Microsoft Office Access 2007.

Scenario:

The number of customers you interact with is increasing day by day. Therefore, you decide to create a database to store essential information, starting with the order and contact details of customers. Also, you want to store the data in related tables so that you can pull out the necessary information according to your specific requirements.

1. Create a new database with the name MyCustomers.accdb.

2. Insert the following fields into the new blank table: ID, ContactID, OrderDate, OrderTotal, and OrderCodes.

3. Save the table with the name tblOrders.

4. Set the data type for the ContactID field as Number, for the OrderDate field as Date/Time, and for the OrderTotal field as Currency.

5. Create a multivalued field for the OrderCodes field with the following values: 0001, 0002, 0003, 0004, and 0005.

6. Create a new table based on the Contacts template.

7. Save the table as tblContacts.

8. Create a relationship between the tblOrders and tblContacts tables, connecting the ID field of tblContacts with the ContactID field of tblOrders in a one-to-many relationship.

9. Save and print the table relationship report.

10. Add the following description to the tblOrders table: *Orders for December 2007*.

11. **Insert a record into the tblContacts table with the following values:**
   - First Name: Carol
   - Last Name: Gordon
   - Email Address: carol_21@abc.com
   - Business Phone: 5852367657
   - Home Phone: 5852667950

Lesson 4 Lab 1

Modifying the Data in a Table

Activity Time: 10 minutes

Objective:

Modify the data in a table.

Data Files:

Contacts.accdb

Before You Begin:

From the C:\084887Data\Managing Data folder, open the Contacts.accdb file.

Scenario:

You are the administrator of a college. You are organizing a class reunion and you have to use a database address book with the contact details of the invitees. You need to find the email addresses of the invitees, add details to the Contact List table when you get contact information of the invitees, delete email addresses that are no longer active, and finally sort the table in ascending order based on the ID and identify the total number of invitees you can contact by telephone.

1. In the Contact List table, **find the email addresses of Venus Rivera and Marcus Coleman.**

2. **Add Andy Gordon's Business Phone number as (509) 555-7688**

3. **Delete Terry Fisher's email address.**

4. **Sort the table in ascending order based on the ID.**

5. **Add a Total row to the Business Phone column in the Contact List table** to identify the total number of phone numbers available.

Lesson 5 Lab 1

Creating and Modifying Queries

Activity Time: 15 minutes

Objective:

Create and modify queries.

Data Files:

Bookbiz.accdb

Before You Begin:

From the C:\084887Data\Querying a Database folder, open the Bookbiz.accdb file.

Scenario:

You are running a book bindery business. Your database includes tables that store information about each book, each order placed, and each customer. You would like to create several queries to answer business-related questions, such as: Which books have sold? How much each customer owes for each order placed?

---

1. Filter data to identify the number of orders placed by Star Base Books.

---

2. Create a query by using the Query Wizard to identify orders for EQ-250 that are over 100.

---

3. Create a query that returns the orders placed between 8/10/2006 and 8/19/2006.

---

4. Create a field that calculates the total price each customer owes for each book order. Change the default calculated field name to *OrderCost*.

---

5. Run the query, and before closing it, save it as *qryBookCosts*.

---

6. Close the database.

Lesson 6 Lab 1

Creating Custom Designed Forms

Activity Time: 20 minutes

Objective:

Create custom designed forms for database tables.

Data Files:

Training Center.accdb

Before You Begin:

From the C:\084887Data\Designing Forms folder, open the Training Center.accdb file.

Scenario:

As head of training at The Music Shop, you use the Training Center database to track students and courses. You need a quick way to manipulate the information present in the database. You will also enhance the appearance and usability of these forms by adding a form title and by grouping and spacing controls.

1. In the Training Center database, **identify and set the relationship between the tables.**

2. **Create various forms** to enter and view data for each of the tables.

3. In each of the forms, **group related controls** to facilitate quick data entry.

4. **Use appropriate form views** to ensure that data is displayed correctly.

5. **Ensure that the tab order follows the logical sequencing of the fields.**

6. **Save and close the database.**

Lesson 7 Lab 1

Creating Reports Using Access

Activity Time: 25 minutes

Objective:

Create reports using Access.

Data Files:

Personnelbiz.accdb

Before You Begin:

From the C:\084887Data\Generating Reports folder, open the Personnelbiz.accdb file.

Scenario:

Your company's employee information database contains basic data about employees, compensation, departments, and parking lots. You want to compile some of this data into various reports. You will use the Report Wizard to create a phone list report based on a query. You will also work in Design view to make some modifications to a report that focuses on the employee payroll.

1. Create a report based on the data in the tblPayAndBenefits table.

2. Save the report as *rptPayAndBenefits.*

3. Apply the Aspect AutoFormat style to the rptPayAndBenefits report.

4. Change the left margin value to 1, and the right margin value to 0.75.

5. Save and close the report.

6. Open the rptParking report in Design view.

7. Change the format of the PayRate control to Currency.

8. Save and close the report.

9. **Create a report using the Report Wizard based on the tblEmployees table.**
   - Add the following fields: EmpID, FirstName, LastName, State, and Phone.
   - Select the Outline layout for the report.
   - Select a style of your choice for the report.
   - Name the report as rptMyEmployees.

10. **Close the database.**

Solutions

Lesson 1

Activity 1-1

1. **Which term is used to refer to a single piece of data?**

    a) Table

    b) Field

    ✓ c) Value

    d) Record

2. **What does the term record refer to?**

    ✓ a) Set of data pertaining to one person or entity

    b) Single piece of data

    c) Category of information that pertains to all records

    d) Group of records stored in rows and columns

Lesson 2

Activity 2-1

1. **In a relational database design, what task is performed after review of existing data is completed?**

    a) Organizing fields into tables

    b) Designating primary and foreign keys

    c) Identifying the purpose of the database

    ✓ d) Making a preliminary list of fields

2. **Why should you enter sample data into tables after creating them?**

    ✓ a) To check for potential data maintenance problems

    b) To identify primary and foreign keys

    c) To create a preliminary list of fields

    d) To review existing data

Activity 2-2

1. **What is wrong with the following statement of purpose?**

The database will have tables for computers, personnel, manufacturers, product, sales, salaries, and company suggestions.

    ✓ a) The statement of purpose should not attempt to list specific tables.

    ✓ b) The statement of purpose is too specific.

    c) There is nothing wrong with this statement of purpose.

    d) The statement does not include statements on what the database will not do.

2. **What is wrong with the following statement of purpose?**

The database will allow the user to generate reports that list the computers used by each employee, as well as queries that sort records by date on which the computer was purchased and the manufacturer of the computer.

    ✓ a) It does not discuss the scope of the database.

    ✓ b) It does not mention or imply how individual entities in the database will be related.

    ✓ c) It discusses specific features (queries and reports) that you would like to see provided.

    d) There is nothing wrong with this statement of purpose.

Activity 2-3

1. **What are the pieces of data from the sample ticket that you think should be included in your database?**

    a) Company name

    ✓ b) Manufacturer name

    ✓ c) Asset tag number

    ✓ d) Department name

2. **What are the pieces of information found on a receiving ticket that will not be necessary to build a database with this statement of purpose?**

    a) Employee's first and last name

    b) Description of the computer

    ✓ c) Employee's hire date

    d) Computer warranty information

Activity 2-4

1. **What additional data will you need to include about each employee?**

   ✓ a) Name

   b) Salary

   c) Date of birth

   ✓ d) Asset tag

2. **What additional fields will you need to include in the database to enable the Technical Services manager and the Finance manager to view the weekly and monthly reports, respectively?**

   ✓ a) Warranty coverage

   ✓ b) Purchase price

   c) Software games included

   d) Configuration of the computer

Activity 2-5

1. **Based on the information you now have, which two tables would be minimally required for this database?**

   a) Computers and Notes

   ✓ b) Computers and Employees

   c) Computers and Departments

   d) Employees and Departments

2. **Which fields will be included in an Employees table?**

   ✓ a) Name

   b) Computer Manufacturer

   ✓ c) Department

   d) Warranty Coverage

3. **Which fields will be included in a Computers table?**

   ✓ a) Asset Tag Number

   ✓ b) Date Received

   c) Employee Name

   ✓ d) Purchase Price

Activity 2-6

1.   **What should be done with the EmployeeName field to normalize data?**

     a) It should be made to list the last name first, with a comma, and then the first name.

     ✓ b) It should be broken up into two separate fields: one for the first name and one for the last name.

     c) It should be made to include the last name data only.

     d) Nothing needs to be done; it is fully normalized as it is.

2.   **True or False? Since the DepartmentName field holds repeated values, a Departments table should hold these values.**

     ✓ True

     ___ False

3.   **True or False? Since not all records have an entry in the Notes field, strict adherence to normalization guidelines would require that the Notes field be moved to a separate table.**

     ✓ True

     ___ False

4.   **What can be done to normalize the data in the ManufacturerID field?**

     a) The entries should all be alphabetic.

     b) The entries should all be alphanumeric.

     ✓ c) Since it has repeated entries, there should be a Manufacturers table to hold that data.

     d) Nothing; it is completely normalized already.

5.   **What needs to be done to normalize the Warranty field's data?**

     a) It should be a text field.

     b) Because some check boxes are not checked, the data is in a separate table.

     ✓ c) Nothing; it is fully normalized already.

     d) More fields pertaining to warranty need to be included in the same table.

Activity 2-7

1.   **Which field needs to be broken down further to the smallest meaningful unit?**

     a) LastName

     b) FirstName

     c) DeptCode

     ✓ d) Address

2. **Based on the data shown, which additional fields would you need to add to normalize the Address field?**

   ✓ a) City

   ✓ b) State

   ✓ c) Zip Code

   d) Country

3. **What are the data normalization problems in this table?**

   a) The LastName field appears before the FirstName field.

   ✓ b) There is a repeated group of Project fields.

   ✓ c) There is a repeated group of Time fields.

   d) The sets of Project and Time fields are not adjacent.

4. **What are the data maintenance problems that this design can cause?**

   a) The project names are too long.

   ✓ b) You would need to edit phone numbers in more than one record.

   ✓ c) Storing only the first name of a person might lead to ambiguity in cases where there are two people with the same first name.

   d) The project naming convention is incorrect.

5. **True or False? You could normalize the data by moving the Project Manager and Phone fields into a second, but related, table.**

   ✓ True

   ___ False

Activity 2-8

1. **Which field in the Employees table would be the most suitable for a primary key?**

   a) LastName

   b) FirstName

   c) DeptCode

   ✓ d) A new field, EmployeeID

2. **In which table should the EmployeeID field appear as a foreign key field?**

   a) Departments

   ✓ b) Computers

   c) Manufacturers

   d) Notes

3. **Which field can be designated as the primary key for the Departments table?**

   a) EmployeeID

   ✓ b) DeptCode

   c) Department

   d) Department Manager

4. **Which table should have DeptCode as a foreign key field?**

    ✓ a) Employees

    b) Computers

    c) Manufacturers

    d) Notes

5. **If you were to add a ManufacturerID field to serve as the primary field for the Manu-facturers table, what other table should have a ManufacturerID field as a foreign key?**

    a) Employees

    b) Departments

    ✓ c) Computers

    d) Notes

Activity 2-9

1. **The values for the DeptCode field have a single occurrence in the Departments table and multiple occurrences in the Employees table. What kind of relationship exists between the two tables?**

    a) One-to-one

    ✓ b) One-to-many

    c) Many-to-one

    d) Many-to-many

2. **The values for the AssetTag field in the Computers table have a corresponding single value in the Notes table. What kind of relationship exists between the two tables?**

    ✓ a) One-to-one

    b) One-to-many

    c) Many-to-one

    d) Many-to-many

Glossary

Access Help

A complete user manual on the functionality of the various features of Microsoft Access 2007.

Access Options dialog box

A dialog box that provides you with various categories of options to customize the Access environment.

AND operator

A logical operator that returns true only if both conditions are true.

arithmetic operators

Symbols used to perform mathematical operations.

ascending order

A sort order that displays data from lowest to highest.

business rules

A set of rules that govern the operations of an organization.

comparison operators

Symbols used to compare two values.

composite key

A combination of two or more fields that uniquely identify a record.

conditional operators

Operators that test for the truth of a condition.

contextual tabs

Tabs with specialized commands that are displayed on the Ribbon when you select an object such as a table, form, or report.

Control Source property

Enables you to set the source property for a new control.

control

An object used in forms and reports that helps the user to interact with the application.

data type

A type of data having predefined characteristics.

database

A collection of information that is logically related and organized so that a computer program can access the desired information quickly.

denormalization

A database performance optimization process that adds redundant data to tables to make queries run faster against very large tables.

descending order

A sort order that displays data from highest to lowest.

existing data

Data in any form that is available for you to be reviewed to check if it falls within the scope of your database.

expressions

A combination of functions, field names, numbers, text, and operators that allow you to perform calculations to produce results.

Field Insertion

A feature with which you can easily insert a new field by typing the field name in the first row of a new column in Datasheet view.

field

A category of information that pertains to all records.

filter

A feature that enables you to filter data based on the data values in a column.

foreign key

A field or combination of fields that contains a value that relates to a primary key field of another table.

form

A graphical interface that is used to display, add, delete, and edit data in a table or a query.

gallery

A repository for elements of the same category. Galleries act as a central location for accessing the various styles and appearance settings for an object.

Getting Started With Microsoft Office Access window

The first window that appears when you start Access 2007. Using this window, you can choose either a blank database or one of the ready-to-use database templates through which you can start working on databases without much effort.

Group By functions

Functions that perform calculations on a group of values.

Microsoft Office Access 2007

A database application used for creating and managing databases.

Microsoft Office status bar

Located at the bottom of the application window, it offers additional convenient features. Using the Microsoft Office status bar, you can switch between different views effortlessly and configure options such as Caps Lock or Num Lock.

multivalued field

A field that is used for storing multiple values.

Navigation Pane

Located on the left side of the Access window, it displays database objects such as tables, queries, forms, and reports.

normalization

A database design process that helps you produce simple table structures free of data redundancy.

NOT operator

A logical operator that reverses the result of a search condition.

Office button

A standard button that is located in the top-left corner of the Access window and forms part of most Microsoft Office 2007 applications.

one-to-many relationship

A relationship between two tables where the primary key of one table has multiple instances of occurrence in the foreign key table.

one-to-one relationship

A relationship between two tables where the primary key and the foreign key are unique.

OR operator

A logical operator that combines the output of two conditions and returns true when either of the conditions is true.

primary key

A primary key is a field that contains unique values, which are used to identify each record.

query criterion

A search condition used in a query to retrieve or manipulate specific information.

Query Design feature

Used to design a query using the Query Design option.

Query Wizard

A feature that helps you create queries using a series of predefined steps.

query

A request sent to a database to retrieve information from it.

Quick Access toolbar

A customizable toolbar that can be used to easily access frequently used commands in the application.

record

A set of data pertaining to one person or thing.

recordset

A table that displays groups of records either from a base table or as the result of an executed query.

referential integrity

The process of enforcing a relationship between two tables that ensures that the existence of a value in a foreign key table is dependent on the existence of a value in the primary key table.

relational databases

Databases that store information in multiple tables, and that can extract, reorganize, or display that information.

report

A screen output of data arranged in an order specified by the user.

Ribbon

A unique interface component that contains task-specific commands that are grouped under different command tabs.

ScreenTip

A label that appears when you place the mouse pointer over a tool. It contains a description of the task performed by the tool.

sort

A method of viewing data that arranges all the data into a specific order.

statement of purpose

A formal statement that defines the scope of a database and helps to guide its design.

subdatasheet

A datasheet that is nested within another datasheet that contains data related to the first datasheet.

Tabbed Document Window Viewing feature

Displays the open database objects such as tables, queries, and forms as tabs in the same window.

Table Properties dialog box

Allows you to add comments about a table. It also displays additional details such as the date on which the table was created and last modified.

table relationships

The association that exists between one or more tables in a database design.

table

A collection of related information arranged in rows and columns.

table

A group of records stored in rows and columns.

Totals

A feature that enables you to add a Total row to your table.

value

A single piece of data.

Index

A

Access Help, 26
AND operator, 133
arithmetic operators, 138
ascending order, 109

B

business rules, 45

C

comparison operators, 132
composite key, 57
conditional operators, 133
control, 164

D

data type, 71
database, 2
denormalization, 49
descending order, 109

E

existing data, 40
expressions, 139

F

field, 3
Field Insertion, 71
filter, 120
foreign key, 58
form, 16

G

gallery, 10

Getting Started With Microsoft Office Access
    window, 6
Group By functions, 144

M

Microsoft Office Access 2007, 6
Microsoft Office status bar, 9
multivalued field, 72

N

Navigation Pane, 9
normalization, 49
NOT operator, 133

O

Office button, 7
one-to-many relationship, 63
one-to-one relationship, 62
OR operator, 133

P

primary key, 56

Q

query, 14
query criterion, 131
Query Wizard, 124
Quick Access toolbar, 8

R

record, 3
recordset, 15
referential integrity, 91
relational databases, 3
report, 17

Ribbon, 8

S

ScreenTip, 8

sort, 109

statement of purpose, 37

subdatasheet, 113

T

Tabbed Document Window Viewing feature, 9

table, 3, 14

table relationships, 62

Totals, 103

V

value, 3

Looking for media files?

They are now conveniently located at www.elementk.com/courseware-file-downloads

Downloading is quick and easy:

1. Visit www.elementk.com/courseware-file-downloads
2. In the search field, type in either the part number or the title
3. Of the courseware titles displayed, choose your title by clicking on the name
4. Links to the data files are located in the middle of the screen
5. Follow the instructions on the screen based upon your web browser

Note that there may be other files available for download in addition to the course files.

Approximate download times:

The amount of time it takes to download your data files will vary according to the file's size and your Internet connection speed. A broadband connection is highly recommended. The average time to download a 10 mb file on a broadband connection is less than 1 minute.